IT'S GOOD TO BE KING

KING HARRIS

CC Imprint

Published by CC Imprint
PO Box 1883, Nipomo, CA 93444
CCImprint.com

ISBN 979-8-9874599-0-4 (hardback)
ISBN 979-8-9874599-4-2 (paperback)
ISBN 979-8-9874599-9-7 (ebook)

Library of Congress Control Number: 2023910529

First Printing 2023

For Sara

Contents

3
THE HOLIDAYS

4
WAR

5
THE NEWS

6
MUSIC

7
PEOPLE

8
SANTA BARBARA

9
SAN LUIS OBISPO

10

OBSERVATIONS

11

EDGAR AND WILLOUGHBY

Introduction

There once was a time, during my youth, when my grandfather had erected a small wooden sign at the entrance to the country road I grew up on in Woodside, California. It read:

Mountain Home Road
Please drive thoughtfully
Look out for memories

Back then such advice was obviously intended for older folk than I, but the message wasn't lost on me entirely. The winding ways of Woodside would eventually lead me to other destinations far and wide, with memories as promised by my grandfather flourishing in the rearview mirror.

I have often wondered how I arrived at today, and who was responsible. Among the assorted and sundry characters I've met in my time, the blame should fall to my family, which could indicate that I didn't have a choice. Seeing how things have turned out, I'm very glad I didn't. Every member of my immediate and extended family always had something to say, some piece of advice to give, some kind of identity and wisdom to share.

Fortunately, most of the time I listened and heard what they said, whether I liked it or not. When I was told to do something, or told not to do something (either directive a kid's nightmare), I usually responded by asking "why?" or "why not?"—risking the usual answer "because I said so," which rarely appeased me or my curiosity.

This is probably the reason I eventually decided to become a journalist, following—I'm proud to say—in the footsteps of my great-great-grandfather, who in the mid-1850s established a newspaper in San Francisco specifically in order to rid the town of a nefarious scoundrel, an act for which he paid dearly.

While my career in journalism wasn't as illustrious or notorious as his, I did manage as a television and radio news broadcaster and print reporter to meet with and briefly chronicle the affairs of some pretty amazing people from all walks of life. And by good fortune I got to write about my experiences, perceptions and observances of one growing up and getting older, which, I'm willing to bet, aren't that much different than yours.

This journey as it turns out is a collection of stories, essays, anecdotes and observations that I have written over the past several years in the form of news accounts and features published in several newspapers, and that I would like to present to you in the form of a book.

It's Good To Be King is a reference to my first name, one that I wouldn't necessarily recommend giving any child under the age of 12. Yet it might be useful later in life if the owner chooses the right profession along with a therapist savvy enough to echo my grandfather's advice: drive thoughtfully and look out for memories, no matter what road you travel.

[September 2021]

I

Family

But it was her laughter I'll remember the most,
along with her spirit, which got us through some
pretty tough times. It can't be easy for a mother to
treat a child with polio, or to see a son off to war.
But she handled such things with grace, dignity,
courage, and kindness. I may still be a wise-guy,
but I know where the wisdom came from.

~ Her Laughter

James King of William; with Ann and James; with Mom; with Dad.

What's In a Name

It's good to be King, but it hasn't always been easy.

Just take the name, for instance. Who in the world would name their kid King? It's a handle that seems to fit better when you are older, but when you're a kid growing up, King is a hard first name to live up to, or to live down, especially amongst your peers. That's one reason, probably, that I was given nicknames: Nicky as a boy, and Nick as a teenager.

My dad's name was King, a moniker he got from his mother, whose maiden name was King. So I too was named King, only I was a junior, but I never used it except legally because no one likes being junior.

My nickname came about after an agreement was reached between my two grandmothers. My father's mother preferred King, naturally. My mother's mother preferred the names of Russian czars, particularly Nicholas. To appease the entire family, it was decided that both names could be used if you spelled King backwards (Gnik with the 'G' silent). So my name would also be Nick.

Apparently it was not enough to traumatize a kid in the first place with a first name like King; they had to come up with a story to explain how I got another, or why I didn't have to use the name King if I didn't want to. Either way, I was cursed with a complex. All throughout my impressionable and formative years, I had to explain my name. You try standing up in front of a bunch of snickering students in a third-grade classroom when your name is called out by a teacher taking attendance.

"Is King Harris, Jr. here?"

"Yes, I am, but my name is Nicky."

"Nicky, it says here that your name is King."

"It is, but I am also known as Nicky."

"So Nicky is your nickname?"

"Yes, and that's what I prefer to be called."

"But King is your real name?"

"Yes, it is."

"Tell me, how did you get the name King?"

"It's my grandmother's maiden name. It was given to my father."

"How did you get the name Nicky?"

"You wouldn't believe it if I told you."

A lot of people, especially the kids you hang around with, automatically think you're arrogant or pretentious when your first name is King. So I chose to use Nicky until I turned 12 and dated my first girlfriend. From then on it was Nick through college, which had its benefits if you liked receiving mail meant for Nick Harris, Detective—a very famous Los Angeles private investigator at the time.

Even when I went to the Vietnam War I went by Nick, although it was against regulations, but that didn't matter because no one in the military ever calls you by your first name anyway. Curiously, it was during this time that a roommate named Ray who bunked with me in Saigon asked me a question one day I hadn't thought about in years.

"How come you never called yourself King?"

"I don't really know. Probably because I didn't feel like a king."

"You mean you wouldn't be accepted?"

"Maybe, and I always had to explain it."

"Maybe it's because you never liked your father."

Ray is now a psychiatrist, I'm sure of it. Whatever the reason, by the time I went back into radio in 1976, I decided to leave Nick behind and become King, but not because it was an effective stage name.

I remember sending an audition tape of my TV news anchoring a few years later to a well-known headhunter in New Jersey named Shirley Barrish. I was looking to move up in my career. Her reply to me after viewing my tape in 1980 is something I'll never forget. She told me over the phone in her thick Jersey accent, "I've seen your tape, honey, and

I gotta tell ya, a king-ga you're not. You won't make it in this business unless you change your name. And puh-leeze! Get rid of the glasses."

Shirley obviously wasn't aware that I had no intention of playing in places like Tulsa, Toledo, or Trenton, but even if I had, I never would have changed my name.

It took me a while to realize it, but King is who I am, and it's good to be King.

[January 2008]

Where Have You Been?

That's a question my mom used to ask me almost every day in my younger years.

Her demand usually was open to interpretation, but seldom mine. Depending on the tone in which she delivered her query, she might have been expressing worry or concern, as if to say, "Why didn't you call me and let me know where you were?" which was reasonable enough, except we didn't have smart phones in those days, and boy I'm sure glad we didn't.

Or after having given me the quick once over, she could have been conveying surprise or even shock at my muddy appearance, that prompted her to add something like, "I thought I told you not to come home by way of the creek."

Or she might display either disapproval or disappointment when I was reproached for not doing something I was supposed to do, chores like clipping the lawn with a manual two-wheeled push-pull mower rusted by rain, or watering all the trees on the property for 20 minutes each, which is an eternity for a kid who'd rather be playing in the nearby streams searching for salamanders or building forts out of hay bales on the Jackling property next door.

The absolute worst to be expected was when her question "Where have you been?" was immediately followed by, "You just wait 'til your father gets home, mister!"

That's about the closest thing to death row that can happen to a kid, worse than the eventual punishment itself.

I suppose I shouldn't have been surprised with such a question; it's easy for a youngster to get lost meandering down country roads exploring the world around him without a care or a sense of time.

As the years went by, as it turned out, my mom (and dad) always knew where to find me simply because of all the jobs I had, initially as an overnight disc jockey, and later as a television news anchor.

If my mom or dad were alive today, both would know they could locate me by turning on the morning news on KVEC radio in San Luis Obispo every weekday from 6 to 9 a.m., but they would be asking "Where have you been?" regarding my weekly appearance in Tolosa Press newspapers, illustrious publications which I'm proud to say I've been associated with (save their first editions) since their inception in the fall of 2006.

I would tell Mom and Dad, as I now tell you, that Tolosa, which weekly prints SLO City News, Bay News, and Coast News, has been undergoing some restructuring during the past year, and was recently purchased by local publisher Bret Colhouer, who tells me he plans to continue to emphasize news, sports, and features dedicated to the communities that his papers serve.

Now that the dust has settled, and having learned the virtues of patience as a youngster from watering all those damn trees, I look forward to continuing to contribute to Bret's enterprise.

This news would, no doubt, have pleased my great-great-grandfather James King of William, the heralded and honored newspaperman and crusading editor who, in San Francisco in the mid-1880s, went after all the unscrupulous ruffians and scallywags who were corrupting the city. He was shot dead in broad daylight at the young age of 34 for his zealous endeavors. His perpetrators were soon caught and hanged by a vigilante committee. With that kind of family journalism in my blood, it's no wonder that I have found myself writing and reporting all these years.

Now that I know where I have been, it may help provide the answer as to where I'm going. And if that's nowhere but here, it's fine by me.

[February 2014]

The Damnedest Thing

I was looking at the list of films being presented at the San Luis Obispo International Film Festival when the title of one of them really caught my attention: *The Damnedest, Finest Ruins* by James Dalessandro.

The film is a much-heralded documentary of the 1906 San Francisco earthquake and fire. "The Damnedest Finest Ruins" is also the title of a very famous and widely published poem written about the disaster back then by my grandfather, Lawrence W. Harris.

I was curious as to how Dalessandro came to choose the same title. Perusing the Internet, I discovered that the talented author, screenwriter, and filmmaker did indeed pick the title from the poem. But I had to know for sure, so I called him up, and he told me something I'd never heard: the mayor at the time might have used the phrase.

"It's kind of a strange quirk that this would happen," he said. "I had no idea that your grandfather had any living relatives or descendants.

"After the 1906 earthquake, it's difficult to say which came first—your grandfather wrote this marvelous poem 'The Damnedest Finest Ruins' because San Francisco was such a majestic city (even in its destruction you could see the hills and the San Francisco Bay) and the mayor of the city at the time, Eugene Schmitz, was also quoted as saying a similar phrase.

"Someone asked him how he felt about the fact his city was completely destroyed, and he said, 'our fair city lies in ruins but those are the damnedest, finest ruins the world has ever seen.'

"After doing some research, it's highly likely that your grandfather coined that phrase and that Eugene Schmitz picked it up from him."

I concur. My grandfather wrote his poem right after the quake and had it first published by A.P. Pierson in September 1906.

And since the history of the famous quake and fire had been such a part of my family's life, I asked Dalessandro why he decided to make it part of his. He told me he couldn't have asked for a better story for a screenwriter.

"It's the denial of disaster, the greatest disaster and the most dramatic event in American history outside of war. All of Northern California along a 300-mile stretch was destroyed from Point Arena to San Jose. It also was the object of the biggest cover-up and lies in American history."

Dalessandro says the death count was much greater than reported, that the Army helped burn the city instead of save it, and no earthquake warnings—which were highly prevalent—were ever heeded.

"It's absolutely an amazing story," he believes. Dalessandro spent 10 years on the project, eventually writing a book and then producing his documentary. He says his film offers new rare and incredible footage before, during, and after the infamous event, an event witnessed and recorded as only my grandfather could have described it in "The Damnedest Finest Ruins."

Of course, my grandfather thought reconstruction was in order, and followed up with a poetic sequel of sorts called "Rebuildin'."

[March 2007]

The Scariest Time of My Life

You don't remember much when you're five years old, but among the few memories I'll never forget (other than Sheryl Adams biting my arm when we were in kindergarten, or riding a horse named Heliotrope in Duncan's Ring, or getting stung by a bee at the Jacklings' pool) was waking up one winter morning in 1952 and asking my mom to take me to the bathroom, to which she replied, "Can't you go by yourself? You've been doing it for several years now."

When she came by a few minutes later, I was, according to her, standing in front of the toilet, shaking uncontrollably. Somewhat alarmed but with presence of mind, she rushed me back to bed, told me not to move, and arranged an appointment with Dr. Williams later that morning.

It didn't take long for Dr. Williams to diagnose my condition. Each time he asked me to walk towards him in his tiny square office, I fell flat on my face.

He looked at my mother and suggested, "Mrs. Harris, has it occurred to you that your son might have polio?"

The very thought must have sent shivers up my mother's spine. Polio, or poliomyelitis, was the most feared and debilitating illness of the time. Its victims were mostly children. The virus attacked the nerves governing the muscles in the limbs and the muscles necessary for breathing. It paralyzed arms and legs, and forced many to live their lives in metal braces or an iron lung machine.

At the height of the polio epidemic in 1952, the year I was infected, 60,000 cases were reported in this country. More than 3,000 died.

It wasn't long thereafter when Dr. Jonas Salk introduced an injected vaccine, followed in 1961 by Dr. Albert Sabin who created the oral version that put an end to the threat and spread of the dreaded disease in this country by 1979.

Of course at first I didn't know what was wrong with me. I thought I had the flu. What I do remember is that after seeing Dr. Williams, my mom and dad wrapped me in a blanket later that night and drove me 45 miles to Children's Hospital in San Francisco.

I was given a spinal tap, in which several nurses held me face down on a table while a doctor poked me with a needle that seemed like it was at least a foot long.

The next day I awoke on a small bed in a quarantined room. I couldn't move from the neck down. That's when I learned I had some kind of infantile paralysis, and that doctors would do what they could short of entombing me in an iron lung.

What they immediately recommended might not have been as frightening, but it was not a procedure I was looking forward to.

Every afternoon at two, a nurse rolled into my room what looked like a cylindrical-shaped washing machine on wheels full of boiling hot towels. After first covering me with a rubber sheet, she then laid steaming towels all over me. Over my screams she would tell me, "I know it hurts, honey, but we have to do it." It was, at the time, all they could do.

The treatment went on for several weeks, but soon I was strong enough to be able to stand, although I needed support. I was to learn later how fortunate I was. It seems I had a milder case of polio than many of the other children in the ward, kids my age who I could now see in other rooms through a window above my bed.

I was in the hospital for a month, and in that time, I had few visitors but had acquired a corner full of toys, games, and stuffed animals, none of which I would be able to take home because of the quarantine. One kind nurse, however, let me smuggle out a Koala bear under my blanket on the wheelchair I rode to freedom.

But though I was out of the hospital, my ordeal was far from over. I still could barely walk.

So every single day for the next six months, while I lay on the kitchen table, my mom would raise my legs to my head to stretch my muscles. I cried because it hurt. She cried because I cried.

But had it not been for those extremely painful exercises, and had it not been for my mother's love, determination, and caring, for which I'll forever be grateful, I wouldn't be walking today.

[February 2007]

Her Laughter

Mother's Day wasn't invented for my mom, but she sure earned her stripes raising the three of us.

I can't speak for my younger brother or older sister, but I'm sure that if Mom were here, she'd tell you that I was probably the most demanding. In that respect, my mom deserved more than a Mother's Day, I think. She should have received some kind of combat pay.

Not that I was a total heathen, but I wasn't exactly the angel she often portrayed me to be to others. I was a rebel, a rascal, and a wise-guy inadvertently searching for new ways to discover some kind of mischief.

Like the time when I was six. I decided for the morning that I'd be mister gas station attendant, so I wiped the windows of my mom's car and filled up her gas tank with water. I knew I must have done something wrong soon after I heard her car sputtering to a stop when she later took off down the road.

Or the time, when I was not much older, that I went into the bedroom with the brand new green carpet that I was told was off limits. But I just had to investigate the contents of a funny-shaped little bottle sitting on her desk, a kind I had never seen before, labeled "Red India Ink." Some of the longest hours of my childhood I spent that day waiting for her to come home.

Of course, no kid grows up without running away from home at least once, and in my case, once would be enough. Whatever the cause on that weekday afternoon—attention, most likely—I bolted, and hid nearby in a secluded grove, while neighbors and friends scoured the countryside into the evening. Consequently, my return a few hours later was met with formidable disapproval and punishment well-deserved. I never ran way again.

But I did try, like other children, to avoid school by being "sick." Mom knew all the tricks, of course. The last time was when I complained of a fever. She had the doctor come over and give me a shot with the biggest needle I ever saw.

I never turned out to be an A student, but I rarely missed a class after that.

Despite all my shenanigans, and there were many more, I have to say my mom was always there for me. And I grew to appreciate that, even the times when she tried my patience as well. Call it payback.

Like the time she tried to cut my hair with what were probably pinking shears, and accidentally lopped off the top of my left ear. The blood and tears flowed until a doctor's advice was applied in the form of a band-aid, which remedied the situation and left future operations to the barber.

Or the time when I was about to leave for the airport to meet my dad to go river rafting on the Rogue River in Oregon, and my brother appeared with a bag of balloons he couldn't blow up. But when I did, my ears popped and my mom thought I was getting the mumps, so the trip was cancelled.

I never knew what the day would be like with my mom, from the time she would dance into my bedroom, always too early in the morning, and fling open the curtains while singing, "Oh, it's going to be such a beautiful, sunny day!" I was hoping for, but knew I was never going to get, any more of the sleep that kids always think they need. Must you always be so positive, so bright and cheery, so full of life, Mother, especially so early in the day?

Of course, she didn't know what I was talking about because that's just the way she viewed the world, from morning until night.

She was incessantly curious, with an intense love of literature, music, history—especially that of California and Native Americans—

and politics. She played the piano and played with puzzles, when she wasn't planting the gardens she grew.

But it was her laughter I'll remember the most, along with her spirit, which got us through some pretty tough times.

It can't be easy for a mother to treat a child with polio, or to see a son off to war. But she handled such things with grace, dignity, courage, and kindness.

I may still be a wise-guy, but I know where the wisdom came from.

[May 2008]

Happy Mother's Day

If you ever want to find out how important and meaningful Mother's Day really is, not that it's necessary by any means, don't do what I did a few years ago.

Somewhere along the line, I got this bright idea to send out Mother's Day cards to all the mothers I knew, including my own mom and all her contemporary child-rearing friends, plus all of the moms from my generation. The list grew to at least 100, far exceeding anything I'd send out at Christmas.

I did this for about five years, and boy was I a popular guy for a while. But the cramps and arthritis that were manifesting in my left hand from all this cursive writing began to take its toll over the years, along with the increasing expense of cards and stamps.

Just as soon as I stopped sending out greetings, I received all these telephone calls or notes demanding to know "Where's my Mother's Day card you always send me? Last year I am a mother and this year I'm not? How could you be so insensitive? Do you know how difficult it has been to raise these children of mine? I've got college to think about. How can you suddenly stop recognizing how much work I've had to do?"

I must admit I was unprepared for the injury—and in some cases the ire—that I apparently caused, but I did discover that mothers are a special and determined breed.

When I think of all the things my mother did for me, I can see why a date on the calendar might be so significant.

If I had a dime for every time my mom took me to the doctor for all the cuts, scrapes, scratches and bruises I suffered, I might be a wealthy man today. She nursed me through a serious bout with polio from which I recovered, for which I'm grateful—one reason why I never complained when she snipped the top of my ear off while she was trying to cut my hair.

She introduced me to history, especially that of California and the Native Americans. If we weren't touring the Gold Country along Highway 49, we'd be traveling to Lassen County in search of the creeks where a Native American named Ishi, the last of his tribe in California, used to roam.

During the summertime, we'd visit either her brother Charlie in Mt. Vernon, Washington, or her brother Tommy who had a house with a beach in Glenbrook, Lake Tahoe. If she had her way, my mom would have driven to either place in a convertible rather than a stuffy station wagon. She was that kind of free spirit. After her divorce from my father, she eventually went out and bought one: a 1961 Chevy Impala.

Wherever she lived, and my mom moved around a lot, our home was always filled with music, whether she was playing piano or listening to classical compositions and Broadway shows. She had a hi-fi system tucked into a large bookcase stacked to the ceiling with novels and other classic literature.

She was always a very curious individual (to the extent of learning the Russian language in 1960—prompting me to ask "Do you know something I don't?"), never failing to impress upon me constantly the value of a good education.

Part of that education occurred outdoors during a couple of Augusts when she sent me to summer camp, which at the mere thought rather repulsed me.

"I don't want to go away to camp."

"Well," she replied, "You're going to go because it will be good for you and because I said so." A command that no kid dare ignore.

"Does that mean I'll be eating camp food instead of yours?" This softened the blow, because try as she might, Mom wasn't the greatest cook in the world, and some of the things she prepared were, well, rather exotic.

To her, spaghetti was goulash; to me, it was Franco-American. She also favored a leathery Swiss steak, liver, shepherd's pie, creamed tuna with minute rice, and Sanka coffee. Any vegetables we ate were occasionally burned, and even when they weren't, what kid likes Brussels sprouts or lima beans anyway?

But Mom was the master in getting you to clean your plate. She'd convince me to eat one lima bean, and after having done so, would comment, "Oh that poor one lima bean. He's going to be so lonely. Better swallow the rest."

Guilt always prevailed. It was just one of the many weapons in her arsenal needed to bring up a kid like me.

[May 2014]

Clean Man

April 9 is my brother's birthday. So I'll call him up, wish him the best, and ask him how it feels to be 61, and he'll reply with something like "You're still older than I am, brother," and then he'll ask me how much I weigh.

He always does when we haven't talked for a while. And since there are no recent pictures of me on his mantle or in his office, I will hedge a bit and tell him I weigh 170 pounds so that he'll have to respond with something like "Boy that's a lot lighter than me. I must weigh about 190 these days. And I was always the skinny kid."

Until the day we both pass on, my brother Jimmy (nee James King Harris) and I will compete with each other, although not as tenaciously as we did when we were growing up.

Sports came easier to me that it did to James, not because I was more athletic, but probably because he was less coordinated, evidenced by one example when he once broke his leg going up a ski slope on a rope tow. And since I was 22 months older and heftier, it was no sweat to toss him around a pool, and I just about always beat him in football, basketball, and baseball, which might have caused him constant despair but only made him more competitive, to such a point that when he finally defeated me in tennis for the first time, his glee and excitement were such that is was as though he had knocked off the reigning Wimbledon champion.

Actually I think all Jimmy ever really wanted was my admiration, and when he didn't achieve that, he tried to get my attention, and in this he succeeded, either by doodling on my bedroom door or in my school yearbooks, or by sacrificing me up to some big errant bully whom he dared that I could beat up.

I decided I was better off if my brother hung around his own friends and got in trouble on his own, which he had no problem doing. Like the time he, as a passenger in his friend Tim Wood's sports car convertible, made a reactive gesture to some young toughs along the nighttime streets of Chinatown, who promptly clomped him on the head with a chain and caused a few stitches, although it looked a lot worse. Or like the time he got into a car accident while visiting Europe one summer, injuring more than his vacation.

Not that Jimmy was born under a bad sign. As a kid his reputation seemed impeccable, at least to our Uncle Larry, who always referred to Jimmy as "Clean Man," a mystical moniker if there ever was one considering he was often anything but.

I think Jimmy was just searching for adventure, like any kid delving in the dirt, and he would find it at various times in his life, either as an apple picker in the orchards of Colorado, or a taxicab driver on the streets in San Francisco, or an advertising man in the state of New York, or a humorous writer with no boundaries whatsoever. All of which led to his current position as director of communications at the lofty Berkshire School near Great Barrington in the western part of Massachusetts.

For quite a while now, this Norman Rockwell part of New England has been home to my brother, his two children, and his wife who goes by the name Shadow. Not difficult to observe here that my brother is also something of a romantic. During his latter college days at Ripon, Wisconsin, so the story goes, James is singing "The Shadow of Your Smile" at a local tavern when in walks fellow classmate Debra Shumar who knows a good tune (at least) when she hears one. Before the night was over, the right chord was apparently struck. Debra was renamed Shadow, and as harmony would have it, they've been together ever since.

All this is quite an accomplishment for the kid I remember coming home one day, totally embarrassed that Linda Hooper, a girlfriend, had given him a black eye.

I'm sure my brother and I will talk about these things when we connect, which isn't as often as I'd like. I'll tell him that, too. I figure that if we spend more time together, we'll have more stories and memories to share, whether it'd be rock 'n' roll favorites or rock climbing along the shores of Lake Tahoe, or playing Marco Polo in the Jackling swimming pool, or cheering Stanford on in the Rose Bowl.

But I'm not going to send him my picture. Then he'll know how much I really weigh.

[April 2009]

A League of His Own

Ty Cobb, Joe DiMaggio, Tris Speaker: legendary major league baseball players all.

But there's another man whose name belongs on this list: my wife's grandfather, William Alexander Lange, Sr. Unless you're a true-blue dyed-in-the-wool aficionado of America's greatest pastime, however, I doubt you have heard of him or any of the monikers he went by, including Little Eva, Big Bill, or The Port Townsend Boy.

Ask any major leaguer worth his stance and he'll tell you that Big Bill Lange ranks among the best, even though he played seven short years just before the turn of the century. Fans who were fortunate enough to see him in action would recall long after he retired his skills as a fielder, his daring base running, and his power at the plate.

Lange also sported a hefty and deadly accurate arm, and his imposing six-foot-two-inch, 215-pound frame earned him at the time the accolade "the fastest big man in baseball."

Lange, who was born in San Francisco in 1871 and ran away to Washington as a youngster to live with his brother Charlie, was only 20 years old when he fielded for the semi-pro Port Townsend Colts. Two years later in 1893 he was signed by the Chicago Colts, a National League club previously known as the White Stockings (ultimately becoming the White Sox across town) that switched to the Orphans until becoming the Chicago Cubs in 1902.

Lange's debut as a rookie was auspicious; he scored 92 times, had 88 RBIs, stole 47 bases, and batted .281, the only time in his major league career he averaged under .300. His stellar performance was no fluke.

In 1895 he achieved his highest rankings by scoring 120 runs, knocking in 98 RBIs, stealing 67 bases, and batting .389—still the top individual season average in Chicago Cubs history. By the time he left the diamond in 1899, Lange's career stats featured a batting average of .330, 578 RBIs, and 399 stolen bases.

For those who dismiss such statistics in the belief that modern day baseball didn't begin until 1900, the game officially hasn't changed since 1893 when Lange broke in, the year the pitching distance was modified from 50 feet to 60 feet and six inches. Except for a new foul strike rule instituted in 1901, the delivery of major league baseball has remained the same to this day.

One sportswriter put it quite poetically many years ago:

> It makes me laugh to hear you guys
> praise modern fielders to the skies.
> When you were tugging rubber nipples,
> I saw Bill Lange drive out his triples,
> and got past second on that hit,
> like Man o' War when feeling fit,
> upon his ear I watched him slide,
> and come up with that old horsehide,
> two hundred pounds of wild mustang,
> in center field was old Bill Lange.

Sometime during Lange's tenure, his teammates dubbed him Little Eva, hardly a nickname suited for two hundred pounds of wild mustang, but apparently appropriate for a gentleman who rarely struck out with women, including his girlfriend Eva, whose constant presence in the press box proved Bill could steal hearts as well as bases.

The charms of another lady many innings later (whose disdain for hits, runs, and errors and whose well-to-do father with equal perception forbade her to marry a lowly baseball player) caused Lange to hang up his spikes at the young age of 28, despite the most lucrative offer from a team at that time.

"I had made up my mind to retire and given my promise to my bride," he told one sportswriter years later. "When Boston proposed ten thousand dollars, I said, 'get thee behind me Satan.' I promised to quit the game, I'm going to quit it, and a little more of this kind of talk and we'll all go crazy."

Little Eva kept his vows and returned to San Francisco where he conquered real estate and insurance, but he continued to be a robust and popular ambassador for major league baseball here and abroad until his passing in 1950, a year after the death of his third wife, Sara Griffith, who produced my father-in-law Bill Lange Jr. in 1928.

Often lauded by sports scribes as "the premiere flycatcher of all time"—he once knocked a plank out of the centerfield wooden fence after catching a liner—Big Bill was considered by his peers to be the best at his position.

Hall of Famer Clark Griffith, owner of the Washington Senators, wrote, "I played with Bill Lange in Chicago for eight years. I have seen all the great outfielders—Speaker, Cobb, DiMaggio—in action, and I consider Bill Lange the equal of, if not better than, all other outfielders of all time."

Connie Mack, the longest serving manager in baseball history, said, "I have seen them all but I have yet to see an outfielder whose all-around ability compares with Bill Lange in his prime."

Big Bill didn't play the required ten years to herald Cooperstown consideration, but he just may be the greatest major leaguer never inducted into the Hall of Fame.

[October 2010]

Flight of the Arrow

When I was a kid growing up, every year on February 14 without fail I'd get a Valentine's Day card from this mysterious stranger who wrote "Will you be my Valentine?" in handwriting I didn't recognize.

The card was always sent through the mail. Of course, if I started making queries into who the sender was, or more importantly who I would like the sender to be, I took the risk of being rejected, which is not a state of affairs any youngster wants to confront.

After a couple of years, I finally solved the puzzle: it was my mom. I guess she figured that getting one Valentine's Day card was better than no card at all. When I asked her about the subterfuge, she replied, "You're not supposed to know whom it came from."

That made sense, I thought, in a couple of ways. First, I wasn't about to admit to all my friends at school that the only person who ever sends me a Valentine's Day card is my mother. Second, I feared that if I acknowledged that I sent a card to a prospective girlfriend, she would, in all probability, after having asked her "Will you be my Valentine?," say "No."

This having been said, it has never surprised me that when someone mentions the St. Valentine's Day Massacre, it's not the vicious 1929 historical Chicago Al Capone bloodbath, or the movies made of it, that first come to my mind. Which is probably the reason I have never personally made a big deal like most people do about this heralded day of love and romance.

Neither has my wife Sara, who has never been fond of the idea of me spending a lot of money for something that will end up being wilted within a few days, like roses. She would rather have a garden.

This I was to discover nearly 30 years ago while I was living in Carmel-by-the-Sea, in a tiny Robinson Jeffers-type cottage with a huge fireplace, small kitchen, tiny bedroom, one bath, and room for practically little else. It was a rental on 10th and Delores, a few blocks from downtown, and within hearing distance of the ocean.

I had taken a job as a midnight-to-dawn disc jockey in Monterey at the time, having parted ways with my first wife, who stayed behind in Los Angeles.

One afternoon, while I was walking to the Carmel Post Office to get my mail, I spotted this beautiful and elegant woman who was working in a travel agency along my route. Definite Valentine material, I thought, until I found out she was married. And when the travel agency moved soon after, it didn't enter my mind that I would ever see her again.

Cupid had other ideas. He was flexing his bow and I didn't even know it.

It was a year before Sara and I encountered each other once again, but she had seen me, because during that time, I had taken a position as an anchor on the nightly local television news.

When she told me her marital situation had succumbed to the same fate as mine, Cupid let go of his dart.

I guess I should have seen it coming. After all, Sara and I had hit it off in brief conversations more than once, were from similar backgrounds and the same Northern California area, and would find out along the way that we knew many of the same people.

So it was little surprise that when we did re-connect, in early 1978, it would be for more than just a moment.

"King, I'm leaving Pacific Grove."

"I suppose you'll be moving back up north," I guessed.

"No. I don't want to move back home."

"Ah, then. Monterey?"

"No."

"Don't tell me you're moving to Seaside," I said.

"No," she replied.

"Where, then?" I asked.

"Carmel."

Hmm. I should have known. Sara had rented a small place not all that far from mine. Translated, that meant that I would inevitably need some closets in that tiny Robinson Jeffers-type cottage with a huge fireplace, small kitchen, tiny bedroom, one bath, and room for practically little else.

Except for a garden.

Which leads me to say that the next time you're thinking about having roses delivered to your Valentine, you may get a lot more than you bargained for.

[February 2008]

2

Growing Up

But I have to say that since the very beginning of
my 40-year broadcasting career, not once has any
prospective boss ever asked me where I went to
college. If they did, I'd tell them Stanford, what the
hell. But I didn't go to the Farm, I went to a small
liberal arts college in Portland, Oregon: Lewis &
Clark. I didn't even know where it was except that
it was at the time about 723 miles from my hometown of San Francisco . . .

~ *Freshman*

Summer Breeze

"OK kids, get in the car, we're leaving for the lake," my mother would cry nearly every August of my childhood.

The kids included me, my sister Ann, and my younger brother Jimmy. The car was usually a station wagon, which the three of us would pile into, and the lake was Lake Tahoe, where my mom's brother Uncle Tommy had a small place in Glenbrook on the Nevada side.

Getting there wasn't always fun—as a matter of fact, it could be quite tedious to a kid who had to stay in one place for ten hours. Freeway construction was under way, and that held up traffic for what seemed like an eternity.

So we mostly traveled on two-lane roads, which was more interesting because we could at least enjoy the Burma Shave signs along the way. This clever marketing gimmick was comprised of five red and white signs stacked several feet apart so you could read them passing by: You can drive / a mile a minute / but there is no / future in it / Burma Shave.

Or: The poorest guy / in the human race / can have a / million-dollar face / Burma Shave. The signs went up in the late forties and lasted through the sixties, until the freeway dictated their demise.

We had other activities: coloring books, 20 questions, card games such as Authors, and identifying other cars on the road (at least they all looked different in those days). And because it was always so hot, we couldn't wait for a Giant Orange juice stand to appear over the horizon.

"When are we gonna get to Tahoe, Mom?" was I'm sure the most irritating question of the trip, asked at least once every hour if not more.

When we finally did arrive, we were greeted by all kinds of cousins, aunts, and uncles, and the strong smell of pine trees that permeated the region. And the beautiful lake, never too cold for a kid who leaps from the car and runs full-steam, skipping the shore and diving headlong into the waters.

Other than swimming, there was a lot to do in the week of our stay. I remember boating a lot in Tommy's green canoe, which he still has to this day I believe. When we weren't water skiing behind the power boat, we'd go out cruising along the shoreline. There's nothing like experiencing the lake from a motorboat.

We also collected planks of wood along the shore and built rafts to navigate around all the rocky points. It was in those rocks where you could find huge numbers of crayfish that were easy to catch. All you needed was a long string with a pebble tied to one end and a piece of bacon. The crayfish scrambled from under the rocks, grabbed the meat with their claws, and were soon delivered to a bucket once we pulled them out of the lake. I never ate them—I only liked to catch them.

Apparently I wasn't the only kid who liked the sport. One summer my sister and I met a distraught mother whose teenage son caught so many crayfish that they filled up all the sinks, bath tubs and toilets in her apartment. Imagine seeing that when you're eight years old.

Of course the time went by quickly, as it does for all kids, but what a way to spend a summer vacation. We were all quite blessed for the opportunity. Uncle Tommy, who is well into his nineties, still visits the place, and when he does, he sleeps at night on the beach under the pines, listening to the waves kissing the shoreline. I wonder what he thinks about every time he sees his green canoe. And when he shuts his eyes at night.

[August 2017]

Summer Camp

Every year about this time, I get calls from San Luis Obispo County camp groups and a press release from the American Camp Association urging that spring is the season to think about summer camps for the kids. It's an annual effort to promote the camp experience for not only young boys and girls, but for parents, too.

Back in my day, the camp experience for my mom and dad was to get the kids out of the house for summer. I always knew I was going somewhere every time my mom started sewing tiny white cloth name tags with my name in red ink on my socks, which made me a bit apprehensive since I was perfectly happy staying at home in Woodside, swimming every day with friends and relatives in Mr. Jackling's giant swimming pool next door and not getting tagged playing Marco Polo.

But my mother was adamant, apparently in the belief that when you're nine years old, it's time to leave the roost. Either that or she needed the break.

"Mom, what are you doing?"

"I'm labeling your socks."

"How come?"

"You're going to camp."

"Camp?"

"It's a wonderful camp we learned about near Santa Cruz, in Soquel. It's in the hills, with lots of girls and boys your age and it's run by a very nice couple. Uncle Max and Aunt Marion."

"But I don't want to go to camp."

"It's called Camp Kennolyn, named after son Kenneth and daughter

Carolyn. You'll learn how to swim, and ride horses, and hike and camp out."

"For how long?"

"Oh, about a month."

"A month? A whole month?" When you're nine, a month is at least a year.

"We thought it would be good for you." That's what parents, especially moms, say just before they revert to their last resort: "Because I said so."

"But I don't want to go to a camp in the mountains with kids I don't know."

"Well, too bad, you're going."

"Why?"

"Because I said so!"

Suffice it to say, I managed, barely, to live through the experience, although I strayed from the trail more than once, and at first had more fun wandering the woods by myself, avoiding some of the scheduled activities.

But my ideas of forestry and those of Uncle Max weren't compatible, as I soon discovered. He and Aunt Marion were not smiling. I was not following the program.

But I survived (as has the camp to this day, by the way) not knowing that four years later, I would be experiencing my second summer outing in the Pacific Northwest on a remote island surrounded by the frigid waters of the Puget Sound—a foreign country as far as I was concerned.

You needed a boat to get to Camp Ta-Ha-De-Wa. No roaming too far off the beaten path here, unless you wanted to brave icy waters filled with 20-foot stinging yellow jellyfish, huge crabs with giant claws, and strong currents. I'm sure Camp Ta-Ha-De-Wa wasn't meant to be any kind of penitentiary, but Alcatraz did flirt with the mind.

Be that as it may, and despite an initial perception of the camp experience that may appear somewhat unenthusiastic, I have to commend my parents for sending me.

It was at Camp Kennolyn on the Fourth of July that Uncle Max, who found out I could recite, chose me to read a passage from the Declaration of Independence in front of the entire camp gathered at a redwood amphitheater in the woods. A great foundation for perhaps a future career in news broadcasting, I'm sure he'd be pleased to know.

And it was at Camp Ta-Ha-De-Wa where I discovered how to endure outdoor activities more strenuous and adventurous than those of my earlier camping days in Soquel, although I still don't know how to throw a Frisbee. But I did learn how to rescue drowning swimmers in the pool and in "the Sound," paddle a wooden canoe hundreds of miles through the Tacoma Narrows to Seattle and back, and build a two-tiered stick birdhouse which I proudly took home to my grandparents.

I even swam around the camp in those icy waters filled with 20-foot stinging yellow jellyfish, huge crabs with giant claws, and strong currents, a feat for which I won Ta-Ha-De-Wa's highest honor: a brass medal in the form of a wigwam. I still have it.

So the next time you see your mom putting your nametags on your socks, try not to get too skeptical, or nervous. Even I can assure you that a summer filled with log fires, shooting stars, and new friends, even mosquitoes, is a great place to camp out.

[April 2008]

Summertime Blues

Boy did I love summertime when I was a kid. I couldn't wait to get out of school.

"Well we'll go swimmin' everyday, no time to work just time to play," was the musical mantra of more than one summer song that encouraged all of us to toss our books and change our ways.

The possibilities for carefree adventure were as endless as the summer months ahead. If we weren't cavorting in a nearby pond or pool, we were flirting with giant sprinklers soaking the lawns, interrupted only by a bee sting now and then, or a call for watermelon and corn.

July wouldn't go by without some kind of camping excursion, and the many days of August were often spent at Lake Tahoe.

As I got older, however, all this summertime bliss would inevitably and eventually succumb to what most teenagers in my day referred to as the summertime blues, and we started dancing to a different tune: "I'm gonna raise a fuss, I'm gonna raise a holler, about a workin' all summer just to try to earn a dollar."

Understand, I had no complaints about earning a buck or two during the summer or otherwise. I was ten when I convinced Emmett Caldwell, owner of Caldwell's General Store, that if he paid me a dime every night, I would clean up the daily mess in the alcove left behind by kids who never put away the comic books strewn all over the benches and floors covered in pools of melted ice cream.

A year or two later I owned the proverbial paper route delivering the Redwood City Tribune all over town.

It was in 1961 when I got my first summer job, at radio station

KSFO in San Francisco, but that was a blast because I got to gopher for the zany and unpredictable morning show comedian Don Sherwood, whose favorite routine was to encourage his drive-time audience to roll down the windows of their cars and turn the radio volume up all the way, at which point he put on a siren, creating one loud and long drone along the Bay Shore Freeway from San Jose to the City.

I should have paid him.

It would be a year later when I would fully realize the summertime blues in June of 1962, when I found myself working at one of those factories where no matter how much money I made to put gas in the car to escort a young lady on a date, I was too dead tired at the end of the day to even think about taking advantage of it.

I don't know if you have ever worked at a lithographing plant, but if you want to learn how to appreciate the value of a dollar, it's a good place to start.

I couldn't get a break, even if I was due one, at A. Carlisle & Sons on Howard St., south of Market in San Francisco. The whistle that blew at eight in the morning was more frightening than any sound Don Sherwood ever put on the air. And more frightening than the whistle was my boss Chuck Wofford, this huge and hefty character with big bushy eyebrows, who bellowed out orders with a Southern accent that made you believe the Civil War wasn't quite over yet.

My job appeared simple enough: I packed labels in boxes that were shipped to food corporations around the country. But all was not what it seemed. I was at the end of a very long, belt- and roller-driven production line. At the other end was Big Mike, the paper cutter with more than one missing finger, who sliced various sized labels meant to wrap around aluminum cans full of fruit or vegetables marketed by companies like Del Monte or S&W.

The labels where then string-tied in bundles by four women further down the line. I quickly learned to adjust, because that rubber belt never stopped rolling. And while it was, I had to choose the right-sized box for the label, mark the box with the correct contents, load the labels into the box in a certain way depending on their size, and place the box in the correct configuration onto a wooden palette. And when that was stacked, I had to drag it to an elevator on the other side of the building.

When everyone was taking a break, I was still struggling with what seemed to be an endless supply of bundled labels. The one and only time I attempted to take a break when the line at my end was momentarily clear, during my very first shift (of course), there was old, crusty Chuck, ambushing me from behind.

"What are you doin' sittin' down?"

"Don't I get a break, too?"

"Don't you ever let me catch you sittin' down, evah. You're supposed to be workin'!"

As Chuck turned and walked away, I made sure he was a good distance beyond before I replied with the only words that came to mind at the moment, and would, for summers to come.

"Sometimes I wonder, what I'm a gonna do, but there ain't no cure for the Summertime Blues."

[June 2008]

Devilish Diplomas

Nothing heralds summertime like the pomp and circumstance provided by the traditional graduation ceremony, where excited and relieved students dressed in gowns let fly their caps in anticipation of what lies ahead, be it the real world, a college or university, a high school, or even a farewell to kindergarten.

Me, I'm surprised I made it successfully out of eighth grade. I'd like to think it was the difficulty of some of the courses taught, like Shakespeare, whose words I can't understand to this day, or algebra and all its theorems about which I couldn't possibly relate.

Maybe it was the austerity of the teachers who believed that since they were instructing 25 bratty kids at a private boy's school, the level of discipline must be elevated.

More likely, truth be told, it was the incorrigible and bizarre behavior of a group of 13-year-old comedians all coming of age (or trying to), who preferred fun and games and tricks to any thought of serious study.

The setting for such a scenario couldn't have been more perfect. For one thing, the square-shaped building in which we were housed, along with seventh-graders separated by a wall, provided all the doors and windows we used for props.

For another, our varied instructors, characters all, easily became our inadvertent victims, or more accurately, targets—except for one giant named Otto Dietrich, the intimidating and overbearing headmaster with hands as big as catchers' mitts, who roamed the grounds all too often, looking for some wayward youngster to slap upside the head.

All other teachers or study hall monitors we considered fair game, and some provided amusement all by themselves without our interference.

Mr. Hodson, for example, addicted to tobacco, never ceased to amaze us with his ability to recite a good portion of Homer's *Iliad* with fumes of smoke coming out of his mouth after one drag from a cigarette.

Pierre Bennerup, who when teaching American history stuttered a bit, made his frustration known every time one of us would finish his sentence. Sometimes when he arrived to teach French, he was greeted by a human chorus of croaking frogs, an amphibious assault that resulted (and deservedly so) in the perpetrators being banished to the boy's locker room.

Mr. "Moon" Mullins, our balding algebra instructor who had served as an Army flyer in World War II, would appear always too early in the morning, draw an outline of Oahu on the blackboard, pinpoint Pearl Harbor, and inform us we were getting a surprise quiz.

Just as fascinating as our teachers were our several study hall monitors, those educators chosen to observe periods other than class, including one who, because he resembled exactly the profile of Alfred Hitchcock, would be greeted by the hum of Hitch's theme song "Funeral March of the Marionette."

Another, Mr. Dean by name, whose acrid breath was caused by drinking chocolate milk first thing instead of brushing his teeth in the morning, prompted any inquisitive pupil to remain less inquiring.

And one monitor whose name I forget, who, upon observing the blackboard emblazoned with hearts and pledges of young love, announced something like, "Ah, Spring must be here! Your something must be twitching!"—which, of course, since none of us knew what "something" meant in those days, led to any dictionary one could find, followed by a collaborative uproar.

While we were scrutinizing the teachers, they were trying to deal with all of us pranksters, who over the course of several months had devised devilish distractions that might interrupt any progress in our strive for scholastic achievement.

In the event of an airplane flying overhead, which was often since we were in the path of San Francisco International, students cried out "incoming" and dropped to the floor.

In the event that someone might be overly flatulent, students were assigned to open certain doors and windows.

Tommy Wilson was the spitball king, and when he wasn't hurling those at the blackboard, all of us were prepared to unleash our Ace bandages across the room at one another when the teacher wasn't looking.

Charlie Nines, already an unruly suspect if only because he endlessly chomped on noisy and stinky Corn Nuts, elected to further his disruptive cause by pulling a string from his desk that rattled a loose wooden slat on the back of a desk chair nowhere near him.

Pete Ready became famous for nothing he designed: Every time in his wingtip shoes he returned a book to the shelves across the room, his stomp would be echoed by the rest of ours, prompting principal Mc-Cluskey, who, while monitoring the seventh grade including students like future deadhead Bobby Weir, stomped himself over to our side in a fury, and, after splintering a door jamb with a well-flung door, threatened us with a personal visit from Otto Dietrich.

Not surprisingly, with that in mind, we all graduated, dressed in suit and tie, and with spirits only a mischievous eighth grader could understand.

[June 2012]

Fountain Valley School

The FBI should be so clever, the CIA so crafty. Neither intelligence agency can hold a candle to the dogged perseverance of the FVS, which has been able to track me down no matter what part of the world I've been in for the past 48 years.

I don't know how the FVS has been able to accomplish this, particularly since I've never given them my address during all this time (even my APO in Saigon during the war), but I'm convinced that if the FVS wants to find you, they will. Bulldog Drummond was never so persistent. I shouldn't be so surprised; the FVS is after my money, always has been, always will be, even after I depart from this earth.

Four times a year since 1962, without fail, Fountain Valley School, a private prep located in the shadow of Pike's Peak in Colorado, has discovered ways to deliver to my doorstep correspondence in the form of bulletins, magazines, reviews, or almanacs, all accompanied by a post script urging alums like me to make financial contributions to insure the school's success in the future.

I think they believe that the sterling education I received there as a high school freshman and sophomore must have eventually led to a career prosperous enough for me to afford a loyal payback or two. So every once in a great while I send a check to my old grey and red alma mater, not so much because of what I was taught but more to applaud the zeal they've exhibited over the years in finding me.

Truth be told, FVS wasn't my first choice for entering high school; at the time in the sixties it was an all-boys boarding operation located in the middle of nowhere down the road from a small town called Security about 40 minutes outside of Colorado Springs. No matter where it was, a high school without girls seemed not only disturbingly uninviting but downright inequitable, but my recently divorced parents figured they could ease their burden by shuffling me off to a college preparatory in the hinterlands, which in the early '60s was how a lot of kids ended up in such scholastic institutions.

I remember one admissions director telling me when I revisited the campus a few years ago, "Back in those days, the parents and only the parents always picked the place. These days, with all the competition between schools, the kids have almost all the input."

Since I did not have any input, in the fall of 1960 I reluctantly packed my bags and flew by prop airplane from San Francisco over the Rockies, naturally apprehensive about the adventure that lay ahead since everything about my new surroundings would be totally foreign to me.

I would soon discover that most of my education would not be realized in the classrooms so much as it would from the diverse personalities of the students and the ripened eccentricities of the professors.

Most of my freshmen or third-form classmates I could relate to (except initially for Ford Bovey and Gordon Yntema, two giant bohunks from the wilds of Montana obviously inducted for the football program who rarely said much and if they did it was in a language I never understood).

I decided to hang around a lot of the upperclassmen because it was they who knew the lay of the land and offered useful tips not included in the official student guide that I considered valuable. Like, since you gotta wear a tie to dinner have a clip-on model handy, or try not to laugh when old Mr. Kitson tries to open his crackers at lunch, or don't give too much grief to the proctors lest they make your life miserable. Proctors were seniors who acted as dormitory supervisors to keep wiseacres like me in check.

When my two drill instructors, Jim Sheridan and Keelty Smith who were stationed right down the hall, seized my deafening record player one night, I immediately replaced it with another I bought from sixthformer Nick Bradley, an exploit not greatly appreciated at the time but apparently admired when it came time to sign my yearbook: "Will you remember me as a sadist?" wrote Jim; "King, sorry for all the trouble we caused you," signed Keelty.

I may eventually have won over the proctors, but the same can't be said for my teachers who demanded the discipline and respect expected as part of the scholastic mission of a private school. Mr. Littell oversaw an exceptionally strict and silent study hall like a marine hell-bent for leather; Mr. Brown had no patience with biology students repulsed by the sight or stink of a frog soaked in formaldehyde; Mr. Rauschenbusch took no guff from lower formers like me who had challenged his authority during a faculty-student softball game.

Mr. Jackson, college advisor and history teacher, advised me, "King, shape up or you are history."

I did, as a fourth-former, thanks to surprisingly prudent counsel from my roommate Jamie Maple, a rowdy El Paso kid who was a bigger jokester than I ever was, which is probably why, along with my loud record player, we roomed together in the first place.

Today Jamie is a district attorney; I'm a news broadcaster. And we owe it all to FVS.

[September 2010]

Fortunate Son

Every time a Friday the 13th rolls around, I am reminded of all things lucky or unlucky, bizarre beliefs, taboos, omens, folklore, and old wives' tales that my mother passed on to me when I was in my formative years. She was a very superstitious soul.

"Now you be extra careful today," she'd warn, straightening my jacket as I headed off to school.

"What for?" I wondered.

"Today is Friday the 13th. It's a very unlucky day."

Friday to me never meant bad luck. I always looked forward to it. It meant the weekend. But I was curious.

"All right, Mother. What's so bad about Friday the 13th?"

"Friday is an unlucky day, and 13 is an unlucky number," she answered, brushing my hair. "If you ever read that Bible you got at Sunday school, you'd know that Friday was the day that Eve tempted Adam with the apple, the 40-day flood occurred, and Jesus died. The number 13 is bad because it exceeds the number 12, which is considered a complete number: 12 months of the year, 12 signs of the zodiac, and 12 apostles of Jesus. Judas was the 13th guest at the Last Supper, and he betrayed Christ. That's why we never invite 13 guests to dinner, and why tall buildings don't have a 13th floor."

She was right, as I later found out, that not only do many high-rises not have a 13th floor, hotels and hospitals don't have any rooms numbered 13. And airplanes have no 13th aisle. So my Mother wasn't the only superstitious character on the face of the earth.

Yet I had a difficult time digesting her diatribe while waiting for the school bus. I began to imagine all the bad things that could happen to me on this dreaded day. Big Bob Kelly was going to beat me up, or I was going to flunk clay class, or that nasty Sheryl Adams was going to bite me on the arm again.

By the end of the day I had survived, although I had to dwell on one embarrassing moment when I stood up in front of the class with my zipper open.

Maybe there was something to this superstitious stuff. There sure was a lot out there, and my mother was full of advice: don't step on cracks in the sidewalk; don't walk under ladders; don't throw a hat on the bed; watch out for black cats crossing your path; don't open an umbrella inside the house; don't let the flag touch the ground; don't give your friend a knife; don't break a mirror; and never harm a ladybug.

Some of Mother's wisdom was handed down through a ritual of some kind. Every time she'd spill the salt while we were eating, she'd throw a pinch over her left shoulder. Bad luck if you don't, she claimed. She avoided using pepper altogether. Spill that, she told me, and you'll have a serious argument with your best friend.

Not all of her tales were those of misfortune. Many of them offered good luck: the proverbial apple a day, the four-leaf clover, the rabbit's foot, the horseshoe, the split wishbone (provided you got the largest piece), and hay bales on a truck, but only if you licked your thumb and pounded your opposite palm with your fist as the truck drove by. And many provided you with dreams come true: wishing on a shooting star, or blowing out all the birthday candles, or knocking on wood. I do remember having a problem with the tooth fairy. I loved getting a quarter under my pillow, but the pain involved in losing a tooth to get it sometimes exceeded its worth.

By the time I got my full set of molars, the tooth fairy was brushed aside, as were most of my mother's fairytales. As I got older, I came to believe in karma instead. You know, what goes around comes around.

Like the time on one April Fool's Day when as a precocious young-ster I filled the sugar bowl with salt, thinking that someone in my family would take the bait. By that evening I had forgotten all about my twisted little prank. I realized this right after dinner when I dove into a bowl of fresh raspberries smothered in fresh cream and covered with what was supposed to be sugar. Never did that again.

Nor would I ever convey a white lie again after one telling episode that occurred while I was visiting my Dad when he was living in Detroit. It was the end of the summer in 1967. I had just gotten out of Navy Reserve boot camp (better than the Army). He was working for an ad agency a few blocks from Motown Records on West Grand Boulevard.

I just had to see "Hitsville U.S.A," home of my favorite music at the time. So I ran down to the Motown offices, shaved head and all, and asked for a tour of their enterprise. When I was turned down because there were no scheduled tours that day, I pleaded with the receptionist. "Please show me around. I may never be here again." Then I pointed to my shorn head and said forlornly, "I'm going to Vietnam in a couple of days." The ruse worked, and I got the grand tour, but it led to another: a one-year tour of military duty in sunny and soggy Saigon two years later.

Be careful what you wish for.

[February 2009]

Number 22

If you are a fanatic of football, be it high school, college, or pro, it's your turn and your time to rock.

As I write this, on this first full college game day Saturday, there are 16 college games being offered on basic cable television (starting with Notre Dame versus Navy at 6 in the morning from Ireland), a slew more if you have a box or a dish, countless others if you download pigskin apps on your smartphone, and several available on radio.

The tailgate season has definitely arrived. And while you gorge yourselves on all those burgers, dogs, and ribs, here's something else to chew on: gridiron days won't be over until early February of next year.

Kind of makes me feel bad for all those wives and girlfriends who must wince when their husbands or boyfriends declare "The season ain't long enough."

I always looked forward to the literal opening kickoff, especially when I started playing the game, much to the dismay of my mother, who thought I was too small to compete, which I was. (Probably one reason I spent so much time roving the sidelines.) She thought I would be pulverized and scarred in one way, shape, or another for the rest of my life, if I survived at all.

My dad's retort was always something like, "Oh, it will be good for him to get knocked around a little bit," which didn't really bother me much until I joined the field with guys who had legs the size of Sequoias and arms that resembled wingspans on B-52s.

I had no idea what position I would be designated, but I didn't care when we got our blue helmets at Menlo Jr. High School. I was so excited—emulating the 49er great Little Joe Arenas, I crudely printed his number 22 in white paint on three sides of it, not knowing of course what number I would be assigned when we got our jerseys a few days later.

As luck, or whatever, would have it, I ended up with Number 22, but I didn't see the action I thought I'd experience. I'm sure the coach was aware of my dad like all other fathers standing on the sidelines anxiously awaiting my participation in our first game, so he threw me in for a couple of downs with an aside to my ear: "Just try to block somebody."

For the reminder of the season, I played sporadically, pretty much seeing nothing but sky after each play, which is why during the following season I was appointed the official water boy for the team.

This setback didn't discourage me from joining the Fountain Valley School "Pup" football squad when I entered my first year of high school. I was deemed a wide and sometimes not-so-wide receiver, since my skills as a lineman had yet to develop.

Much to my surprise, and most certainly that of the coach, I caught the ball for the very first touchdown we scored through the air. Having thought I had found my niche, I became a starter, until I was injured a few games later. Some defensive clown tackled me square in the knee and bent it backwards, sending me not to the sidelines so much as to the hospital.

Now donning crutches instead of a helmet and pads, I vowed I'd return the next year, which I did, but not as a receiver. As a sophomore, despite my slight weight of 130 pounds, I centered for the quarterback on offense and played defensive end when the opposition had the ball.

The Danes (as we were known for our mascot), turned out to be a pretty accomplished football team, due for the most part to a cagey quarterback named Keith Ballinger, who after faking a run, lofted long passes to speedy receiver Mark Minthorn who was more familiar with the backfield of our opponent than they were.

And I must admit that it was a rare feat when any opposing half-back tried to run around the area I was there to protect, despite my playing with a split lip for most of the fall—an injury I wore as proudly as Henry Fleming in *The Red Badge of Courage*.

But despite a successful season, I wasn't about to continue on in my brief gridiron career. Upon glancing at the size, the speed, and the ferocity of the varsity squad, I decided it was time to hang up the old cleats. Getting knocked around was one thing—getting pulverized was another.

Looking back, overall I had a pretty good time. But I can't say I was unhappy when the pigskin and I parted ways.

[September 2012]

Freshman

One of my favorite jaunts of the early fall is walking through the streets of downtown San Luis Obispo to experience Cal Poly's Week of Welcome. You can usually spot the freshmen pretty easily with their inquisitive eyes, apprehensive faces wearing that certain smile of adventure encouraged by parents in tow.

They had nothing like WOW when I went off to college for the first time. As a matter of fact, I'm amazed I even got into one.

During high school, Dad had drilled me on accomplishing two things: going into the military of some kind, which I rejected since Vietnam was beckoning, and getting a college degree. Why? Because your future employment may depend on it.

But I have to say that since the very beginning of my 40-year broadcasting career, not once has any prospective boss ever asked me where I went to college. If they did, I'd tell them Stanford, what the hell. But I didn't go to the Farm, I went to a small liberal arts college in Portland, Oregon: Lewis & Clark. I didn't even know where it was except that it was at the time about 723 miles from my hometown of San Francisco, long before the construction of I-5. And I didn't know that freshmen weren't allowed to have cars.

No matter. Leaving my high school sweetheart behind, with no cell phone or GPS, I packed up some clothes (but mostly my records and my stereo—I was way into music) and loaded it all up in my '56 Chevy coupe and headed north to the Winter's cutoff above Sacramento.

From then on, it was two-lane blacktop except in a couple of stretches all the way to the Siskiyou summit at the Oregon border. I figured the drive would take about 13 hours, mostly because I had to stop in every small town along the way, plus I had to fight for a roadway jammed with big rigs traveling north and south. I was beginning to think that this was some kind of death journey.

Traffic eased up a bit once I passed Red Bluff and Redding, where I had enough space to breathe and take in the beauty of the golden and red fall scenery. So this is what it's like going off to college, I thought to me, myself, and I. Going off to college began to take on a new meaning.

I finally landed in Portland that night, found a motel, and prepared myself for a meeting with a dean the next morning. He's going to ask you about your car, you dummy. Better think of an answer. But I didn't have to as it turned out. He assumed that, like all the other freshmen, my parents dropped me off.

My other apprehension was who my roommate would be. As I would find out, he was from Portland, certainly a blessing with my having little to no knowledge of the area. And he, Justin, had a car, which he could leave at home.

After unpacking, Justin looked at me quizzically and asked, "Haven't you got any clothes?"

"No," I said, "just records."

Little did I know that Justin liked music just as much as I did. Within a semester, he would join the college choir and start up a folk trio. Not only that, he and I would later join forces to create a rock 'n' roll band.

I asked Justin the day I met him, "Do you know what your major is?"

A rather silly question, I thought, since I figured how could anyone 18 know what he wants to do.

"Insurance," he replied, without skipping a beat.

As for me, I had no idea what I was going to study; Western Civilization was not relevant in my world at the time. But music was. Before I even went to an advisor for any educational direction, which is one of the first things a freshman is supposed to do, I had discovered that L&C had a campus radio station in a dilapidated building next to the gym.

With Top Forty and rock 'n' roll on my mind, I entered the small facility and met Daryl, a very square student station manager who politely informed me that KLC broadcast news, sports, and serious music (meaning either folk, classical, or jazz).

"What?" I cried. "No Beatles?"

The burrowed frown that came over his face told me all I needed to know. "We are looking for a DJ to fill the 3 to 5 p.m. weekday slot. It doesn't pay, and I don't know if anybody listens to it. Interested?"

"Sure!" I shot back, guessing that Daryl was one of those non-listeners. "I'll even supply my own records."

Not long after I started my disc jockey stint at KLC, the station began ordering weekly Top Forty singles, which was music to my ears. Not only had the format changed, but KLC moved to a brand new location. And by the fall of the next year, the school offered its first class in radio.

I won't take credit for developing a new curriculum, but my first year in college was worth the drive.

[September 2016]

The Old College Try

Message to all college graduates who are about to enter the real world (although if you're reluctant to do that I will understand): Congratulations on getting your degree; it's a grand accomplishment you won't soon forget.

I know I haven't. I still have nightmares about it.

First of all, I'm amazed that I even got into a college, much less finished one. As early as the sixth grade I realized all I ever wanted to be when I grew up was a rock 'n' roll disc jockey. To Jerry Lee Lewis I could relate; to Shakespeare I could not. And I figured that since I had spent most of my time listening to a transistor radio glued to my ear I might as well get a job that pays me something for doing it.

My parents were, of course, horrified. Even though I graduated eighth grade, they still feared the worst, that I was on my way to becoming some kind of juvenile delinquent. So they shuffled me off to a prep school somewhere deep in the vast snowbound plains of Colorado.

Two years later, realizing I could get Cs for free, they whisked be back to my hometown high school just long enough to transfer me to a college prep academy. My parents were determined to determine where I'd be for the next four years. I remember them telling me in unison in no uncertain terms in my waning days as a senior, "You will go to college and you will broaden your horizons."

"Mom, Dad, can I have my radio back?"

"No," again in unison.

Having no other recourse, I applied to several small liberal arts colleges in the Pacific Northwest, and got into them all to my amazement, considering Colorado. I was leaning towards Lewis & Clark in Portland. I had done a little research and found out they had something the others didn't: a campus radio station. That's all I needed to know.

I was elated when I got accepted, but apprehensive at the same time, since I was never known to be the scholarly type.

Vergil Fogdall was apprehensive, too, apparently. Then Dean of Admissions, he typed up my acceptance letter, stating at the top, "It gives me pleasure to inform you that the Committee on Admissions has been favorably impressed by your credentials and has approved your admission." Although what credentials I had was as much of a mystery to me then as it is now.

I was ecstatic, nonetheless, until I got to the bottom of the letter and saw Vergil's personally penned caveat in blue ink: "College level work will demand of you your very best, King, but if you will accept the challenge, we think you can be successful in it."

That I pondered. I could probably avoid taking a class on Shakespeare, but not Chaucer, who was even harder to understand.

"We believe you can do it, son," said my very delighted father, who, with acceptance letter in hand, added, "The success of your career, my boy, will depend upon your college education."

Thanks, Dad, for the encouragement. Nothing like a little pressure, especially on a 17-year-old who had little clue about what he was going to do with the rest of his life, except perhaps that he desired to spin platters.

So naturally the first thing I did when I arrived on campus, even before I went to my assigned dorm, was make a beeline to the radio station, located in an antiquated shack behind the gym. I opened the door with K-L-C stenciled on it. A real straight-looking kid wearing a jacket and tie introduced himself as the program director. Beethoven was blaring from the studio.

"Hey, does this station play the Top Forty?"

"What's that?" he answered. I took a deep breath and sighed. You're right, Vergil, I thought to myself. This is going to be a challenge.

But for every class Lewis & Clark required me to take, like Western

Civilization, or psychology, or Chaucer, I seemed to find courses more suited to my style, like broadcasting, or speech, or oral interpretation. While none of these was offered as majors, I was unknowingly honing skills I would need later on, writing various copy and logging programming for KLC, along with introducing to an unsuspecting student body the latest rock 'n' roll hits of the day.

Vergil must have been inspired. I was doing my very best. But it wasn't easy.

It took me a few courses my final summer to pass the ultimate grade required to enter the real world, so I missed commencement. But I did graduate, with a B.S. degree, which amuses me to this day.

[June 2009]

3

The Holidays

We were not a wealthy family by any means,
despite any appearances, but in many ways we were
richer than most, if only for that one precious
November day we all shared. For that I am grateful,
as I am for the road we traveled to get there.

- Giving Thanks

Giving Thanks

I grew up in sunny California, but my family and I always celebrated Thanksgiving as though we were living in the snow-covered peaks of Vermont.

As we took the annual November trek to my grandfather's house in San Francisco from our house in Woodside 40 miles to the south, all of us in the car—Dad, Mom, bother Jimmy, sister Ann, and I—would sing out our favorite ode to Thanksgiving, written by Lydia Maria Child in 1844: "Over the river and through the wood to Grandmother's house we go, the horse knows the way to carry the sleigh through the white and drifted snow."

Our sleigh was a station wagon, and although there were plenty of woods and creeks in Woodside, there was nary a river or snowdrift. Yet we continued onward for the hour it took in the frosty autumn air, all bundled up in our Thursday best, chanting about "blowing winds stinging the toes and biting the nose" until our collective breaths eventually fogged up the windshield.

Thanksgiving at the modest Pacific Heights home of Lawrence W. Harris on 3445 Washington Street was more than a family tradition; it was considered by some to be a seasonal obligation, where the patriarch of the clan (L.W. or "G" as we called him) required the attendance of his three children, Lawrence II, Robert, and my father King, along with all their wives with all their children, plus numerous great aunts and great uncles, assorted old family friends, and any other non-familial visitors who otherwise might be left out in the cold.

It was a close-knit crew for the most part, if only because the living room wasn't all that spacious for such a large flock of festive folk who gathered not so much to honor the turkey as they did to pay allegiance to my grandfather.

While he was sitting on his throne, not far from a cozy fire fueled by coal, his wife Lucy, the matriarch of the clan whom we referred to as "Grams," never sat still, flitting like a busy bee from one flower to another, greeting and mingling with all her guests, making sure everyone's glass was full, glowering at all the exuberant children running around should any of them misbehave, referring people to their assigned seats at all the various dining tables, and orchestrating the meal being prepared in the ovens and on the stovetops.

I can unequivocally state that observing my grandmother on Thanksgiving Day was like watching pure theatre on a Broadway stage. I would have gone over the river and through the woods to her house if only to experience how she conducted all the cooks in the kitchen, who I learned later were informed that it would ultimately be she who would be taking credit for roasting the birds.

Turkey with stuffing of course was not the only fare to grace our plates or our palates; all the trimmings associated with a Thanksgiving feast were served, including a most delicate dish I'll never forget, one that could have only been created in the forties and fifties: creamed San Francisco cracked crab surrounded by a ring of wild rice. The sweetened hard sauce that accompanied the desserts was also a family favorite, but that's most likely because (according to my mother) it was laden with rum.

Grownups anticipating this blessed bounty all took their places around a long oak dining room table showered by the glow of candlelight and decorated with an autumnal cornucopia of rusty-colored fruits, flowers, and flavors only a fall season can provide. Children sat nearby at cloth-covered card tables set up for the occasion and scattered around the living room.

Soon the gaiety, laughter, and cheerful chatter temporarily succumbed to the solemnity of the moment when grace was spoken and thanks were given before the turkeys were brought out to be carved—a ritual and duty, by the way, approached with some apprehension by all three sons who boasted cuts of perfection when in reality their skills with a knife left much to be desired (in particular those of my father, whose reputation for butchering a bird was such that I often stepped in to help him out). After all, there are only so many times a fowl cutter like my father could ask, "Would anyone like a piece of dark meat?" before people got the idea that he was more than hesitant about having to perfectly slice the white.

And while the gravy was being passed around, anyone whose fork was not needed at the moment used it to strike the side of a water glass several times to get everyone's silent attention, introducing the array of toasts and signaling the clink of wine glasses that were to follow well into the meal. And in the Harris household, toasts and clinks were as plentiful as the food on this afternoon.

Most of the praise and gratitude—well deserved—went to Grams and G for giving birth to the family, and then bringing all of us together over the years in what I always believed turned out to be one splendid spectacle.

We were not a wealthy family by any means, despite any appearances, but in many ways we were richer than most, if only for that one precious November day we all shared. For that I am grateful, as I am for the road we traveled to get there.

Want directions? You know where to go: over the river and through the wood.

[November 2008]

Bloated Blessings

I don't know about you, but Thanksgiving to me these days has become somewhat of a conundrum.

For reasons beyond my imagination, family members far and wide who can't stand each other most days of the year load the car or pack the plane on Wednesday with everyone else on the planet in a furious scurry to get to grandmother's house on Thursday to overstuff themselves with an uncomfortable afternoon meal that could feed the population of any Third World country, while watching football on last year's television set which will probably be replaced by this year's model at 4 o'clock the following morning after another furious scurry to the nearest Black Friday mall hawking the cheapest deal.

Cynicism aside, there was a time when I always looked forward to Thanksgiving because as much as it was a time to count blessings, it was also an occasion that usually provided more entertainment than a circus. And with the nutty family that I had, there was never a dull moment—but plenty of sharp blades.

"What have you got there, Dad?"

"This is the year I'm gonna do it, son, you just wait and see," he exclaimed, beaming with excitement. He had just returned from the local hardware store, totally unfamiliar territory for my mechanically ham-fisted father, who as everyone agreed was always better off drinking a screwdriver than using one. So I was surprised to see him so elated.

"Just look at this!" he shouted, pulling from a box what must have been the first electric carving knife ever made. "This year, the turkey is mine," he crowed.

"Darn," I replied, frowning.

"Something wrong, son? Aren't you happy for me?" he asked.

"Well, if that thing actually works, I suppose I'll be a little bit let down. I hate to admit this, Dad, but the highlight of my Thanksgiving is watching you butcher the bird and listening to you curse the entire time you're doing it."

"Sorry, son, but this year's gonna be different." And, as promised, it was. He cut the cord.

Can't blame my dad. He never did get much practice separating the white meat from the dark. He didn't have to, thanks to his two brothers.

Long before the advent of the electric knife, all of our Thanksgivings were held at the home of my Edwardian grandfather, who demanded that every November his entire flock and then some be in attendance so he could baste in the glory for having sired a vociferous brood that included three very talented and competitive sons, two of whom always volunteered to carve the two turkeys, usually because by the time it came to take up the scalpels they appeared to be as roasted as the birds they were about to slice.

This tradition ended with the departure of my grandfather, resulting in subsequent celebrations family-wide, such as a few with my dad, and one I remember with my older sister that was scheduled to take place but never happened because her big birddog named Nemo figured out a way to get into the outside refrigerator where a turkey destined for the oven found itself instead as a feast for a hungry hound.

Somewhat miffed by the experience at the time, my sister wouldn't give it a second thought today since she is a devout vegetarian, and will relentlessly remind you of that fact should you prefer to dine either on what grazes on the ground, flies through the air, or swims in the sea, with what could be construed as a condescending remark that goes something like "I don't—and you shouldn't—eat anything with a face on it."

My stepdad Tom Collins had no problem digesting a well-cooked turkey, and that he did quite literally when he visited our household one Thanksgiving Day soon after my mom passed on.

I had decided to barbeque a bird for the first time in my life and in looking back I should have notified the local fire department as soon as I lit the coals. An hour hadn't even gone by when Tom couldn't recognize the appetizer he was nibbling on, wiping tears from his eyes caused by all the smoke spewing forth from the grill. Never one to mince words, the former Army aviator bellowed, "You know where there is smoke, there is usually fire," which there was, much to my mortification.

After extinguishing what was little more than a toasted carcass (and my pride as well) I tried to convince him that a blackened and crispy fowl was the latest rage, but he wasn't buying it. I was just relieved that he preferred dark meat.

One final thought: However you spend your Thanksgiving Day, do try to leave enough room for grace. You can't get too bloated on the blessings we all have.

[November 2009]

Father Christmas

Christmas has got to be a tough time for moms and dads, if for no other reason than finding ways to perpetuate the legend of Santa Claus to us kids in various stages of our development.

Mine, for example, would throw me and my younger brother in the car with my older sister in tow and travel to San Francisco to visit Kris Kringle at The White House department store, just to prove, I suppose, that he did indeed exist. Plus they would point to the half-eaten cookie and half glass of milk we'd left out for Santa on Christmas Eve. But try as I might, I could never quite buy into Old St. Nick's visit to our house, as depicted in Clement Moore's Yuletide ode "A Visit from St. Nicholas."

"'Twas the night before Christmas, when all through the house, not a creature was stirring, not even a mouse." Wrong. My not-very-mechanical dad was forever stirring, trying in vain to put someone's bicycle together. As for mice, we had too many cats.

"The stockings were hung by the chimney with care, in hopes that St. Nicholas soon would be there." With care meant not using nails, screws, duct tape, or superglue.

"The children were nestled all snug in their beds, while visions of sugar plums danced in their heads." The last thing I'm sure a kid wants from Santa is a sugar plum. Would have made life easier for my father, though.

"And mamma in her 'kerchief, and I in my cap, had just settled our brains for a long winter's nap." Not dad, continually cursing over that darned bike.

"When out on the lawn there arose such a clatter, I sprung from the bed to see what was the matter." There was clatter all right, from the garage. Dad just dropped his toolbox again.

"Away to the window I flew like a flash, tore open the shutters and threw up the sash." Dad desperately hoping for a mechanic?

"The moon on the breast of the new fallen snow gave the luster of mid-day to objects below." No doubt my dad's screwdrivers, wrenches, ratchet sets, and pliers.

"When, what to my wondering eyes should appear, but a miniature sleigh and eight tiny reindeer. With a little old driver so lively and quick, I knew in a moment it must be St. Nick." This makes sense. My father, after all, was in advertising.

"More rapid than eagles his coursers they came. And he whistled, and shouted, and called them by name: Now, Dasher! Now, Dancer! Now, Prancer and Vixen! On, Comet! On, Cupid! On, Donner and Blitzen! To the top of the porch! To the top of the wall! Now dash away! Dash away! Dash away all!" And all this time I thought it was Dad swearing.

"As dry leaves that before the wild hurricane fly, when they meet with an obstacle, mount to the sky. So up to the house-top the coursers they flew, with the sleigh full of toys, and St. Nicholas too." Please, Santa, make one of those toys a bicycle for Father's sake.

"And then, in a twinkling, I heard on the roof, the prancing and pawing of each little hoof. As I drew in my head, and was turning around, down the chimney St. Nicholas came with a bound." Not likely. Our chimney was akin to a pipe. I looked.

"He was dressed all in fur, from his head to his foot, and his clothes were all tarnished with ashes and soot. A bundle of toys was flung on his back, and he looked like a peddler just opening his pack." Ashes and soot? Impossible. Dad could never light a fire, either.

"His eyes—how they twinkled! His dimples how merry! His cheeks were like roses, his nose like a cherry. His droll little mouth was drawn up like a bow and the beard of his chin was as white as the snow." Did I tell you my dad was an art director?

"The stump of a pipe he held tight in his teeth, and the smoke it encircled his head like a wreath. He had a broad face and a little round belly, that shook when he laughed, like a bowlful of jelly. He was chubby and plump, a right jolly old elf, and I laughed when I saw him, in spite of myself." Ad-man Dad always chuckled when he saw a commercial opportunity.

"A wink of his eye and a twist of his head, soon gave me to know I had nothing to dread. He spoke not a word, but went straight to his work, and filled all the stockings, then turned with a jerk. And laying his finger aside of his nose, and giving a nod, up the chimney he rose." By this time I'm figuring there's something in the milk we left behind.

"He sprang to his sleigh, to his team gave a whistle, and away they all flew like the down of a thistle. But I heard him exclaim, 'ere he drove out of sight, Happy Christmas to all, and to all a good-night." Come Christmas morn, there were three bikes under the tree. Maybe I should re-think all this.

[December 2010]

Just the Facts, Ma'am

The story you are about to read is true. Nothing has been changed to protect my innocence.

June 1954. It was foggy in San Francisco. I was working the day watch out in my backyard. I needed some sun. Then my dad came home. I was about to get a break . . .

"Dad, you just gotta take me with you. I just gotta meet him!"

I had just found out my father was traveling to Hollywood to visit with an advertising client of his, and I thought that if I could just get down there, I figured chances were good that I might meet up with my absolute (and nearly everybody's) favorite TV hero at the time, which, in my case, for reasons I still haven't understood and really don't want to, happened to be a bigger-than-life cop.

I was so elated when my father told me I could go that of course I didn't hear him when he cautiously advised me that it probably wasn't going to happen. My ears perked up however when he admitted, "I don't have much pull with television studios, son."

To which I countered, "Dad, just take me to the police station." Which he did.

So here I am, seven years old, in the lobby of the Los Angeles Police Department, standing almost at attention before a towering wooden desk occupied by a wrinkled and gruff old desk sergeant who either had a bad breakfast that morning or wished he were still on patrol.

"What do ya want, kid?"

"I'm here to see Sgt. Joe Friday."

"Who?"

"Sgt. Joe Friday. I see him every week on *Dragnet*. He wears badge 714."

"Kid, you yankin' my chain? You know what happens to little boys who fool around?" he threatened, pointing with his nightstick to the JAIL sign.

Unfazed and determined, I cried, "He's just gotta be here! I came all this way to see him. Can't you call him or show me where his office is?"

"I'll tell you one last time, sonny. He ain't here."

"Well, maybe he's in robbery detail. Sometimes works homicide. He gets around a lot. He hangs around with that fat partner of his, Frank Smith? Maybe they're not working the day watch today. They might be on night watch."

"OK, buster," growled the crusty constable, leaning over his desk, staring me into the floor, making me feel like I'd just committed mass murder. "I'm only gonna say this once. Sgt. Joe Friday ain't here. You know why he's not here? Because Sgt. Joe Friday doesn't exist. There is no Sgt. Joe Friday. Never has been, never will be. He's just an act on television, kid. Happy now?" He smiled malevolently, then sitting back down, muttered, "Now quit wastin' my time."

I couldn't believe what I'd just heard. I felt like someone had pulled the rug out from under my feet. I was speechless for a moment until I gathered enough courage to respond. Standing my ground and pressing my luck, I glared back at the curmudgeon in blue and exclaimed,

"I suppose the next thing you're going to tell me is that there is no Santa Clause!"

I shouldn't have provoked him. When he looked up and returned my dare with that malicious grin of his, I knew it was time to leave. I wasn't about to be Scrooged twice.

As disappointed as I was for the moment, I still knew where I could find Sgt. Joe Friday, even if he didn't pace the halls of Parker Center.

But I wasn't about to be toyed with over the existence of Kris Kringle. I had always been certain he'd be headed my way the instant I opened the first December day of my advent calendar. Nonetheless, I felt some kind reassurance might be in order, having just experienced devastating news that might arrest anyone's belief. So as soon as I got home, I thought of peppering my mom with questions about Santa Claus, like Sgt. Friday would with a witness or a suspect.

I opted instead to revisit an old newspaper clipping my mom read to me when I was younger. It was the response in 1897 by Francis Church, editor of The New York Sun, to eight-year-old Virginia O'Hanlon, who had written him asking "Is there a Santa Claus?" The partial prose that lifted my faith:

> *Yes, Virginia, there is a Santa Claus. He exists as certainly as love and generosity and devotion exist, and you know that they abound and give to your life its highest beauty and joy. Alas! How dreary would be the world if there were no Santa Claus. It would be as dreary as if there were no Virginias. There would be no childlike faith then, no poetry, no romance to make tolerable this existence . . . No Santa Claus! Thank God he lives, and he lives forever. A thousand years from now, Virginia, nay, ten times ten thousand years from now, he will continue to make glad the heart of childhood.*

That's all the proof I'll ever need and I'm sure that's all the evidence that a cop like Sgt. Joe Friday might require.

I can just hear him say, "All we know are the facts, ma'am."

Merry Christmas.

[December 2009]

Weathering the Holidays

I don't know about your Christmas celebration, but I hope it was as inspiring and joyful as mine.

There was a time in my life when I used to shake and shudder at the thought of getting together with certain members of the family during the holiday season. You know, the outspoken well-oiled uncle or the born-again stepmother proselytizing in tongues.

Those days of angst and expectations are long gone, I am pleased to report, as are the months and years of miscommunication and indifference.

Today my immediate family, aside from my wife Sara, includes my older sister Ann, who lives in Greece, my younger brother James who with his wife Shadow lives in Massachusetts (and who spawned two children, now adults), and my stepsister Lynn, married to Bruce and living in Northern California.

All, except James, I haven't seen or talked to in years, a situation I suppose I could blame on distance, but in this hectic day and age of technology, that wouldn't stand up in any court.

So this year we all decided to put away any and all baggage, and meet up with one another on Ann's 75th birthday at a Thai Restaurant in Mill Valley, California, much to the delight of birthday girl Ann, who adores Asian food (which she can't ever find in Greece but still hasn't forgotten how to order—which was of great benefit else we all would still be there today trying to figure out what to eat).

Ann flew in from Greece, James couldn't make it, which made him extremely envious (as he is prone to get whenever he misses a family occasion, especially this one), but Lynn did arrive, along with several cousins from my father's side of the brood, and Ann's daughter Elizabeth.

We didn't have a lot of time, but all of us recognized each other and made strong connections, catching up after a lengthy passage of time. It really was a marvelous reunion, with nary a resentment as might be expected in some family get-togethers—simply complete abandon and acceptance.

Following good-byes and well wishes, that night we celebrated the Yuletide with Sara's side of the family at her father's house in nearby Larkspur. This event was made special by the appearance of Sara's younger brother Art, who had been somewhat estranged from his father Bill for the past two years, so their meeting took a significant turn for the positive.

As usual, Bill's wife Susan, who is also an accomplished gourmand, provided the holiday feast, which was consumed rather quickly by other members of the family including son Sean, his partner Lenora, and Susan's sister Karen. But it was more than gratifying to see Art and his father together again.

Since my sister Ann was spending more than a week in Northern California, I had the opportunity of spending time with her the next day. We had a terrific time, talking about our childhood in the country-side, our parents and their ensuing divorce—which caused a tremendous rift and other negative consequences—and our lives after that.

Considering what all of us went through, not just in my family but in Sara's as well, I can look back and realize that we all turned out reasonably well. Now that I'm getting older, I have begun to understand how important families really are, especially for the support they can offer, even if they live in another country of the world.

I asked Ann why she chose to live in Greece of all places.

"I toured the area several years ago, and did like Portugal a lot, but for some reason I just ended up in Greece," she said. "You must come over. It's beautiful. You can swim where I do in the summer," pointing her finger at a picture of the Mediterranean shoreline.

I just might do it, and bring her some Chinese food.

Sara and I headed home, with rain all the way down from Larkspur to Arroyo Grande. As I saw the wiper blades attacking the windshield, I thought about how cleansing it was.

And how we managed in the same way to conquer the stormy weather of our past.

[December 2016]

New Year in Style

Every New Year's Eve, in the days during World War II and several years after, a celebratory gathering would take place at the Spanish-style mansion of one Daniel C. Jackling, a gentleman who in the early part of the last century became rather wealthy by discovering a new method of mining copper.

His multi-acre estate prominently featured a multi-roomed several-storied manor entangled in bougainvillea, a six-car garage with servant quarters aloft, a vast carpet of religiously watered and mowed green lawn dotted with oak trees that seemed to extend as far as the eye could see, a bath house built not far from a giant swimming pool saddled by tiled brick and surrounded by hedges as high as an Iowa cornfield, and a professional tennis court. A myriad of pathways led to one of many colorful gardens and a hothouse or two, and several dirt roads would eventually wind their way to either a dairy operation or an animal farm that was more like a zoo.

This is the way I remember it as a youngster growing up right next door to the Jacklings. They were good friends of my grandparents, who sold my parents three acres of their property, which was located in what was then the very rural town of Woodside about 40 miles south of San Francisco.

It was no surprise that the Jacklings had become the center of our social activity, especially during the summertime, when my parents along with their post-war suburbia-entrenched friends (plus all our relatives) would gather around the Jackling swimming hole to create memories that still exist to this day.

I was too young to attend the heralded Jackling New Year's Eve celebration, but a black and white photograph taken in 1948 reveals the revelry of what looks like quite the evening. Below it in the frame are the signatures of all the guests—dressed to the nines, the men decked out in fancy tails, the women wrapped in gowns that sparkled from the glow of baubles, bangles, and beads required only by the formality of the affair, a custom of the times.

Not one of the 100 or so attendees is portrayed without a festive grin, fueled no doubt by the passing of the previous year and the promises of the one coming in, but as well by the generous flow of spirits, good tidings, and cheer.

Pictures, of course, cannot render properly the gaiety of the conversation nor the variety of music that accompanied the evening, but I can assure you that short of having Guy Lombardo and his Royal Canadians appear in person to provide a very personal rendition of "Auld Lang Syne," the Jacklings were well-suited to livening up any affair with melody and harmony.

In the sunken living room where everyone got together was not only a piano that was always busy, played by whoever sat down to musically contribute to the evening, but also an enormous pipe organ, which required the expertise and talent of a maestro to bring it to life. According to those who attended year after year, what came out of that pipe organ on New Year's Eve could lift Daniel Jackling's house right off the hill on which it was built.

The Jackling home is silent now—has been for years. Not long after his death and that of his wife, the property was subdivided. What was left, the Jackling mansion, was eventually bought by the late Apple founder Steve Jobs, who battled the Woodside City Council for years to have the Spanish-style adobe torn down. With his passing, the fate of Daniel Jackling's Woodside palace is still in limbo.

Pictures of the estate today show that since it hasn't been lived in for decades, it is in great need of repair. But in its glory days, the estate was brimming with life and vitality, where people gathered together on a summer's day for a swim, a game of tennis, or a romp through the sprinklers, or bonded together on a cold wintry night that rushed in a New Year with elegance and style, acknowledging an appreciation for the past, and offering a hopeful gesture to all the families representing the future.

Happy New Year to you all. And it's perfectly all right with me if you want to celebrate it like you have a huge pipe organ.

[December 2011]

Happy New Year!

Oh. Forgive me. I just realized my enthusiastic salutation—HAPPY NEW YEAR!—might be a bit too acute for those of you who may have excessively celebrated the demise of a year that was already not unlike a bad hangover.

So for that I apologize, and will do my best to keep any further bold or capital letters to a minimum to keep your aching head from pounding any further.

I wish I could offer a cure for the uncomfortable condition in which you find yourself, but alas, I cannot, because (and I know you don't want to hear this, especially at any volume, high or otherwise) there really isn't one, despite the amazing advances of science.

It's too late to tell you how to prevent the ultimate curse of the spirit world now that you've hoisted on high one glass too many, accompanied either by the strains of "Auld Lang Syne" played by Guy Lombardo and his Royal Canadians, or the beat of Dick Clark's *Rockin' New Years Eve* (which always gave me a headache even without alcohol).

Since the time has passed for me to offer any advice on how best to minimize the damage (like prefacing your party with a glass of milk or a tray of hors d'oeuvres, or drinking vodka or gin instead of bourbon or red wine along with the copious amounts of Gatorade required to keep you from dehydrating), I can only pass on a few remedies that might alleviate some discomfort.

I am, however, reluctant to guarantee results.

If your head feels close to exploding, like it's center stage to that Jimi Hendrix experience performed at the Monterey Pop Festival in

1967 where he kneels over his guitar all ablaze after fretting the most amazing version of "The Star Spangled Banner" ever electrified, you're probably in need of some kind of painkiller. That would be aspirin, but medicos agree that while this might somewhat relieve the ache, it can inspire your stomach or liver to further revolt *en masse* more than they already have.

If your brain feels more bruised than battered, like it has entertained one too many choruses harmonized by The Carpenters, then it's your own darn fault for listening to them in the first place.

I might suggest a fizzy concoction, but that has its perils. A World War II veteran of my acquaintance once recalled being stationed in Britain when, after a night of revelry, he offered a white tablet of this particular medicine to an English comrade unfamiliar with the remedy. He swallowed what looked to him like a large pill with a glass of water, which immediately caused him to writhe around on the floor with foam coming out of his mouth, prompting him to believe (and frantically vocalize between burps) that his American buddies were out to get him, much to their hilarity and his chagrin.

I could also recommend, as some people do, that you consume a sturdy grilled and greasy bacon, egg, and cheese sandwich, but frankly (just between you and me), the thought of trying to digest that kind of payload the morning after anything I find kind of nauseating anyway (and I'm sorry for using any word stemming from nausea, given your current dilemma).

Perhaps you might try a shot of fructose or glucose, which can be found in a can or bottle of tomato or orange juice, but then you may feel tempted to graze the proverbial hair of the dog by adding to either of nature's nectars the vodka that brought on your hangover in the first place. And while the procedure is sworn by in some circles, many say it just exacerbates and prolongs your suffering.

You might want to avoid coffee, by the way, because all that does is dehydrate you further and wake you up enough so you not only realize just how much pain you're in but also reminds you of the evening before, which I'm sure you'd just as soon forget.

If there is a banana on your kitchen counter, or any vitamins in your medicine cabinet, or a jar of honey in your pantry, you haven't got anything to lose by swallowing any or all, as any or all may aid you in your quest for relief, but you might want to think twice before experimenting with home remedies like skullcap tea or the extract from certain artichokes (that is, if you can think at all).

Ultimately, I'm afraid time is the only tonic, and sleep the only antidote.

Hopefully you'll awake to a more joyous and prosperous new year, one that proffers not only a cure for the hangover we all seem to have, but to all of mankind's current ailments.

HERE'S TO THE NEW YEAR! Oh. Sorry about that.

[December 2009]

4

War

This is going to be a most pleasant experience, I thought: teaching 17-year-old Vietnamese navy recruits—and I'm sure some Viet Cong infiltrators —absurd refrains like "Please pass the bread" and "The rain in Spain falls mainly on the plain" while a war was going on in one of the most humid climates on earth in a building that could easily be toppled by a single car bomb.

~ *It's All Greek To Me*

With students in Saigon, 1969

Post-War

I remember growing up my parents had a lot friends. Most of the men had served in World War II, and some managed to have children during that time, usually in 1941, 1946, and 1948.

Post-war had lured them to the suburbs, in this case from San Francisco to Woodside, at that time a small country town on the peninsula about 40 miles south of the city. I found it peculiar that most of the dads worked in the city and chose to trek back to the country, but that's what you did in those days, I guess.

Another peculiarity I noticed was that very few of these soldiers and sailors talked about or mentioned their war-time experiences. At least to their children.

My father, for example, after graduating from Stanford, joined the Navy Reserve after the war broke out. Little did he realize, it was the reserves that did much of the fighting in both theaters. Dad's first duty was as an ensign for an LST (landing ship tank) that brought supplies to the islands in the Pacific.

His next tour of duty was during the waning part of the war, when the desperate Japanese started using Kamikazes, which he as a commander told me later was the most frightening part of war.

I learned, as he got older, when he was ready to share his experiences, of the crisis he faced during this period. As his ship was approaching Mindoro, his fleet was attacked by a wing of Kamikazes. His best gunner, who happened to be in the brig at the time for some indiscretion, was immediately called to quarters to man a gunnery detail, and shot two Japanese out of the sky, saving Dad's ship. He always told me that it wasn't he who was a great leader, but that he had surrounded himself with really great people. That's a pretty heady thing to admit. Being in the Vietnam War myself, I understood exactly what he meant.

As kids, we rarely knew of the horrors service men like my dad endured. If we asked, they didn't want to talk about it much. As a matter of fact, nobody ever did, to me anyway.

When all of the parents and us kids got together for a gathering, which was often, the last thing anybody thought about was the war. No wonder. It was finally over after years of struggle. Time to forget and put the past behind. Look ahead to the future.

The gatherings were great. While all the kids spent time playing Marco Polo in the local watering hole, the parents picnicked nearby. We're talking about 30 parents here, and all of their offspring.

I don't like saying this, but most if not all have passed. Which is a shame, because they were all such fine and caring people. And the sacrifices they made were enormous. The war notwithstanding, raising a family is difficult enough.

My dad eventually entered the advertising world, and he and Mom raised three kids who to this day still share stories with each other. That is more than a blessing.

Just as much, I get to talk to all those kids I grew up with. The stories are amazing. And for that, I have to thank their parents. And mine.

[September 2017]

Lessons Learned

War isn't something you usually think about while walking the streets of downtown San Luis Obispo in the fall sunshine, unless perhaps you happen to be sauntering past the old Bello's Sporting Goods storefront on Monterey Street, where that striking memorial to U.S. troops who have died in Iraq is on display.

As I recently paused to survey the faces of the more than 1,000 servicemen individually pictured on the wire grid, hundreds of new Cal Poly students being wowed and wooed were passing by, most I'm sure unaware that there but for fortune, their fates might be linked to a war being fought far away, as it was when I was going to college.

Back then, with the Vietnam War raging in the mid-1960s, college students could be drafted into the Army unless they retained a grade point average of C or higher. So many were being deferred that the Selective Service System deviously devised a nationwide test in the summer of 1966 designed to snag students no matter what grade they had, to satisfy the never-ending thirst of the Pentagon for more troops.

The SSS was so desperate at the time it even enlisted blind people, one of whom I recall responding at the time, "Gee, this is great! I always wanted to be a bombardier!"

Suffice it to say, I didn't pass the test, but the repercussions weren't felt until I had already begun my junior year at Lewis & Clark College in Portland, Oregon. My mother called me from our home in San Francisco at 7 o'clock one weekday morning in October, telling me I was "1-A" (no longer deferred) and that I was to report to the Army in two weeks.

Up until this point in my life, Vietnam was just a protest, not a life-threatening reality.

I was stunned, flabbergasted and scared to death. I didn't mind serving my country, but I wanted to do it on my own terms. What to do?

Following my father's footsteps and advice, I opted for the Navy Reserve program, which, if I could get in, might at least allow me to finish school. I also hoped it might keep me out of harm's way, although I couldn't count on that knowing my father had sailed against the Japanese in World War II.

I immediately scurried over to nearby Swan Island in Portland to the chants of "Good Vibrations" blaring from my car radio. The Navy Reserve outfit there, although they had openings, wouldn't take me because they said I had to serve near my hometown. So I drove the 723 miles to Treasure Island in San Francisco, where I was told they couldn't sign me up because I went away to school in Portland and wouldn't be able to attend the mandatory monthly meetings. "Go back to Swan Island," they suggested. So I drove the 723 miles back to Swan Island, only to hear, "Your home base is Frisco. We're not going to take you." I turned around, drove another 723 miles, and upon my return to T.I., falsely announced I quit school and was ready and eager to join.

I would not be officially sworn in until the following July, but at least the Army was off my back, and I could finish college, which, unbeknownst to my reserve unit, I did, although every month during my senior year I had to fly to San Francisco from Portland on my own dime to make those mandatory monthly reserve meetings.

I managed to avoid war overseas for the time being, but not the war at home; with a short military haircut, I no longer found any peace amid the long-haired protesters during the infamous "Summer of Love." The sacrifice would be worth it, though I thought being a "weekend warrior" I might avoid river patrol in Southeast Asia when the time came for my active duty.

Wrong.

While I was waiting to board my reserve ship for a two-year tour in San Francisco Bay, the Navy discovered my recent English degree and deemed me qualified to teach Vietnamese navy personnel how to speak our language so we could train them how to operate our watercraft soon to be left behind.

I spent a year in Saigon.

War is one hell of a thing to have hanging over your head while you're trying to get through college. I hope that students who pass by the memorial on Monterey Street realize just how fortunate they are.

[September 2006]

It's All Greek To Me

Want to know what I find terribly amusing? The rise in popularity of Dual Language Immersion programs, where young students are taught both English and another language simultaneously, when not too long ago many "patriotic" Americans were demanding that immigrants who don't speak the English language don't belong in this country.

Even more ironic is the fact that students who enroll in the program will end up speaking and mastering two languages fluently, an aptitude those same "patriotic" Americans have never achieved.

This controversy of course doesn't exist in places like Europe, where it's common that almost everyone speaks everybody else's language. Frankly, I admire anyone who can speak more than one language, if for no other reason than that it's a practical and often necessary means to understand someone else's culture, something that too many "patriotic" Americans fail to pursue—one reason why I believe Americans are considered so arrogant and condescending by the rest of the world, and why we endlessly fail in winning over the hearts and minds of peoples whose countries we invade.

Take Vietnam, for example, where much to my surprise I found myself immersed in language training. In early 1969, as a member of the U.S. Navy Reserve, I was waiting for my active duty orders, which I thought would entail a two-year stint as a yeoman on board a destroyer based in San Francisco.

But the Navy people in Washington had different ideas, since the 1968 Tet offensive had politically changed our course in the war. This led to a program called "Vietnamization," whereby U.S. forces would turn over our military machines to the South Vietnamese, and that would require language training so all could effectively communicate during the exchange. What the Navy needed then, like the Air Force and the Army, were language instructors.

They decided that the best teachers in this endeavor might be gleaned from college graduates like me who had degrees in English. How they came up with that correlation always astounded me, since reading Mark Twain or Shakespeare hardly qualified anyone for such a noble purpose.

Nonetheless, when my orders finally arrived, I learned that any dreams I had about sailing around San Francisco Bay on the USS Twining for two years was not going to happen, and I was eventually shipped off to the Defense Language Institute at Lackland Air Force base in Texas, where I would be taught how to teach South Vietnamese navy personnel our language—nuances, idioms, and all.

"Wait a minute," I said to one of my DLI professors. "What makes you think I'm a teacher?"

"You were an English major, weren't you?"

"Yes."

"You know the language then, don't you?"

"Obviously, but I've never taught before, and I can assure you, I don't know a lick of Vietnamese."

"You don't need to know any Vietnamese, just English, and we'll show you how to teach that."

"But how will they know what I'm saying to them if they don't understand what I'm saying?"

"Listen, smart guy, just follow the instructions in this manual, and be thankful you're not a grunt."

Six weeks later, I found myself in downtown Saigon, working in a dilapidated and very vulnerable nine-story building with one stairwell and three classrooms on every floor (save the ninth, where there was a laboratory with rather crude audio tape machines with earphones attached).

This is going to be a most pleasant experience, I thought: teaching

17-year-old Vietnamese navy recruits—and I'm sure some Viet Cong infiltrators—absurd refrains like "Please pass the bread" and "The rain in Spain falls mainly on the plain" while a war was going on in one of the most humid climates on earth in a building that could easily be toppled by a single car bomb. Actually I'm surprised it wasn't, especially after the two-story Air Force school nearby was flattened several weeks after I arrived in-country.

Considering the absurdity of the situation, I was not surprised to discover that the very first English word I was to convey from the first page of the Army manual was "thanks," but there was one minor problem: my students could not pronounce it. No Vietnamese could enunciate, much less string together, "th" or "nk" or "ks." How's that for Army know-how?

So I threw out the book, and discovered that just about the only way to effectively communicate with my foreign naval colleagues was either in terms of money (a universal language that nearly everyone understood) or to a few by speaking French, which I could "parle un peu."

I'd like to think I was successful in my language immersion technique, if you will, and perhaps may have even saved a few lives. We would have saved a heck of a lot more, though, had we understood their language, and their culture, in the first place.

[May 2012]

Vietnam Revisited

Every year about this time, I occasionally think back to the Vietnam War. It was July of 1969 that I went over there, and I'd be there for a year until I could come back to "The World."

Despite my status as a deferred college student and a Navy reservist, in 1968 I graduated with an English degree, and that's what got me boots on the ground.

Vietnamization was part of a new policy that saw Americans handing over equipment and supplies to the South Vietnamese, who also needed to learn how to speak English so we could train them for the transition. So, since I had a bachelor's degree in English, the Pentagon thought I would make an excellent language instructor.

When I heard I was being ordered to Saigon, I gave the Navy my opinion of the idea, telling them this was one of the dumbest concepts I ever heard of. You don't go off to a war zone to teach kids another language; it won't work, I told them.

All my Navy and Air Force pals at the Defense Language Institute at Lackland Air Force Base in San Antonio felt the same way, not that our complaints made any difference. I felt compelled to show the brass, for example, that the Vietnamese would never be able to pronounce the word "thanks," one of the first terms issued in the Army manual. They can't enunciate TH-AN-KS.

Having got no thanks for my observations, after six weeks we arrived at Ton Sa Nute.

I got there ahead of my language pals and went directly to a Navy office to find out where I'd be billeted. I was immediately ordered to put on a rank flak jacket and dirty helmet, grab an M-14 rifle, and make myself useful on guard duty.

"Guard what?" I asked. (The building had been bombed five days before I got there.)

Although Tet the year before had depleted the Viet Cong to a large degree, the war was still raging, which prompted me as soon as I got to my permanent quarters to ask a Marine, "Hey, you've been here a while. How safe is it here being a blonde, blue-eyed U.S. Navy seaman wearing jungle green and sporting an M-16?"

"Safer than New York City," he quickly shot back. Well, THAT made me feel better.

After having protested America's role in Vietnam during four years in college, it quickly became apparent that I was right in concluding that the South Vietnamese government was corrupt.

Take the black market, for example. It's all around you as soon as you get there. If you couldn't find American goods at the local PX (a military-style Costco of its day) you could find anything you needed on the streets. And if you did find something at the PX, like Cognac, you'd simply leave it in the cab taking you back to your barracks and the cabbie would pay you four times what it was worth.

Currency exchange was a joke, and on a larger scale, any much-needed supplies meant for the field went to corrupt commanders who literally stole entire ships.

All this of course wasn't the only assault to your senses; it was hot and humid, malodorous, noisy, and downright dangerous. I was not even there for a month when the Air Force language school was blown up by a suicide car bomber. It never occurred to me that English teachers could be such a threat, but we were, apparently, and would be for the entire tour.

The most worrisome fear was that you didn't know who might be the enemy; you couldn't trust anyone. If, for example, you were out at night and stopped by the "white mice" (Saigon Police), they would threaten you with jail time unless you paid them whatever you had in your wallet.

So new recruits in-country spent the nighttime on the rooftops, smoking pot and listening to "Suite: Judy Blue-Eyes" being delivered over Armed Forces radio.

The lifers, meanwhile, invaded the bar scene and tore up the joints, getting in fights or receiving wicked diseases from way too many prostitutes. Guess who went to LBJ (Long Binh Jail) for such behavior? The potheads, of course.

It was going to be a long year.

[August 2015]

Dream On

Had the weirdest nightmare the other night. I dreamt that Congress, in order to shore up our fractured military war machine, and knowing full well a draft would incense and inflame all mothers who'd then put a stop to all wars which would be considered un-American, decided to call up all tried, true, and tested Vietnam Vets to solve the problem.

Why not? Who better to pass on such armed expertise to young soldiers fighting for freedom and democracy in Iraq and Afghanistan, right?

Our gallant troops, we were led to believe, in trying to fend off communism in Southeast Asia were, after all, deadly in their aim to search and destroy, successful with winning the hearts and minds of the people, and experienced in victory on the battlefield. Not only that, they are familiar with guerilla warfare, landmines, booby traps, tanks, helicopters, AK-47s, faulty armor, borderline sanctuaries, corrupt governments, greedy contractors, and illicit intelligence agents, cover-ups, and certainly drugs.

No matter if they don't know the Afghan language or understand their culture; neither does anybody else. And although the location is different, turning in jungle fatigues for desert camouflage is an easy enough trade. But, alas, the bar girls will be in short supply. Our vets will just have to adjust. Thank God we ignored the noble French or we wouldn't have such a reserve to draw upon.

Continuing this dream, I remember interviewing three former combat veterans before they took off on a night flight out of Travis

Air Force Base headed to the Middle East. Duty-bound soldiers as they were, they were understandably quite reluctant and skeptical.

Mortensen was the first to speak up. "We could show 'em how to win the battles but I ain't showin' 'em how to lose the war. I'll let the politicians do that." Mortensen was a drafted Army grunt from New York who relentlessly pursued the illusive Viet Cong through high grass and low lands for a year and was surprised he made it out alive. He had to convince himself that his odds of spending the same amount of time in the desert, like the delta, were still probably better than surviving some sections of the Bronx for 12 months.

Aframe wasn't as confident. "Not that I'm hesitant or anything, but I gotta tell ya, I hate these damn wars when you don't know who to shoot at. I mean, God forbid if you kill a civilian." In his days when Aframe was toting around an M-60 in hamlets where frightened villagers bowed to Charlie at night and Americans by day, the giant Montanan often shot first and asked questions later. "Can't do that these days. You'll get reamed by the general." The general Aframe was referring to was a concerned Stanley McChrsytal, overseer of U.S. forces in Afghanistan, who recently acknowledged to the world, "We have shot an amazing number of people, but none has ever proven to be a threat."

"Nice, huh?" Aframe responded. "I'll feel right at home."

"So will I," admitted Mortensen. "With all the land mines they got over there, we won't have a leg to stand on." Nobody laughed, but a joke was needed.

That's when the fatalistic former sergeant West quipped, "What the hell, let's just get 'em all stoned. They have enough opium." West, an opportunistic and gung-ho G.I. all spit and polished for the adventure, was given a purple heart in Saigon after being run over by a troop truck on his way to a dope deal. "Count me in, gentlemen, if there's money to be made," he said, maybe not so facetiously.

"Hey, West," countered Mortensen, "that's one reason we lost our war, too much corruption. We gotta stop throwin' money at a government nobody believes in."

"Yeah," chimed in Aframe. "What will we be fightin' for anyway? I could kinda understand goin' after the Commies."

"The way I see it is simply like this," offered West. "We train the Afghans, rout the Taliban, and salute the flag of our newly installed and trusted government. Then we leave."

"What about al-Qaida?" asked Mortensen.

"Somalia, Yemen, Florida maybe, but at least they won't be in Afghanistan," answered West.

"Doesn't sound like a very workable plan to me," said Aframe. "Too many lives, too much money. We've tried this before. What if it doesn't work?"

"You're not doubtin' me, are you, Aframe? For one thing, this all comes down to national security," West stoically asserted. "Nobody's protesting like the last time. For another, the media will buy into whatever we tell 'em. Or don't tell 'em."

"Not lately," countered Aframe. "Two videos I saw the other day showed an American chopper gunning down two journalists in Iraq, and an Army cover-up of innocent civilians being mutilated in Afghanistan."

"People always forget," argued West. "None of that's going to be investigated. Besides, there's a My Lai or two in every war. I'm tellin' ya it's going to work."

"Maybe," figured Mortensen, "as long as we don't ask the Russians."

At this point my alarm woke me up, but I don't think that's the last of my nightmare.

[April 2010]

Memorial Daze

If Memorial Day represents a day of reflection, which I think it does, there is no better mirror than the Vietnam Veterans Memorial Wall.

The first time I saw the Wall was from the air, as our jet passed over the mall on a late winter afternoon in 1985 on its way to land at Ronald Reagan Airport in Washington D.C. Those who told me it would resemble a giant scar on the landscape weren't that far off the mark. But how appropriate, I thought—a wound to America's pride, certainly, but one meant hopefully to heal.

I was invited to make the journey by University of California Santa Barbara religious studies professor (and eventual Congressman) Walter Capps, whose moving and singular course on the effect of the Vietnam War in America was just beginning to receive nationwide attention and would eventually occupy a segment in a future CBS *60 Minutes* program.

What made Capps' class so unique was not its content or even its premise, although not many historians at the time were as visionary enough as Capps was to look at America's worst military defeat as a "positive event" in how we could learn from it.

Capps' class literally grew into something profound as local Vietnam Vets began to seek it out as a safe haven to peel back their scars, open up their wounds, and recount their painful experiences for the first time since their return to a country that up until then not only refused to recognize their sacrifice and achievements but labeled them murderers as well.

Very few vets were willing in the 1970s—and even the decade

beyond—to publicly admit they had served in a very unpopular and losing campaign. It was not by design, Capps once told me, that more and more vets who started hearing about his class began to show up to take the stage of Campbell Hall's 900-seat auditorium to reveal their secrets to a generation that knew little about it. For the first time, their courage and heroism were acknowledged and appreciated.

For the spellbound students, this was an unexpected and unparalleled course about life and death, suffering and sacrifice, resolve and redemption. That prompted a design to take it a step further. Capps began to select students from his class, and along with a few now-familiar vets, started making an annual pilgrimage to Washington to visit the Vietnam Veterans Memorial Wall.

Being a Vietnam Veteran myself and having already reported on Capps' class and the Vietnam veteran situation in Santa Barbara for TV station KEYT, it seemed necessary to record the next phase of the story: where by personally experiencing the Wall, UCSB students whose fathers or uncles were involved in a conflict they would rarely talk about might better understand the rage, depression, futility, and silence that still simmered in their souls far beyond the battlefield.

I knew going in that the controversial Wall was not the typical monument to fallen warriors, but I wasn't expecting it to be so overwhelming in such a subtle way.

It did not stand above the ground, but was sunk into it. As I gradually walked the path alongside the reflective black granite panels, focusing on the more than 58,000 names engraved on that wall, I found myself slowly descending towards the center of the wedge-like structure into what felt like a coffin. Before I realized it, I was standing below the apex, ten feet above me.

For every name I studied, I could see myself in the reflection.

To my right, in the distance, I could see the Washington Monument; to my left and much closer was the Lincoln Memorial. Down in front of me, and all along the 500-foot pathway, were hundreds of flowers, pictures, letters, and other sentimental treasures, many providing a glimpse into the story behind the name. And if these didn't tell a tale,

I heard one from just about everyone I bumped into with every panel I passed: some cried, some laughed, some swore. More than a few held in their hand a rubbed-on pencil etching of a familiar name inscribed in the stone to take back home.

One quiet soldier I met staring intently at a few names told me he was there to say goodbye to members of his squad who never made it back. "Why them, and not me?" I heard him whisper, in somewhat of a Memorial daze.

"I don't know," I replied. "I wish I had an answer for you."

Then he turned to me with a painful look in his eyes, "Did we really all do this for nothing?"

"Look around. I don't think all these people here at the Wall believe that. I think they're saying thanks. And welcome home."

[May 2017]

Peace with a Price

Philosopher Bertrand Russell once said, "War does not determine who is right—only who is left."

I share his opinion. Having lived through one in Vietnam, I am fortunate, but the carnage it left behind was catastrophic. A case in point: more than 50,000 Americans died in the war, and almost as many vets since then have committed suicide. Post-traumatic stress is a battle unto itself.

This I again realized in the late fall of 1988 when I made a journey halfway around the world to document the dilemma of Soviet soldiers having returned home from Afghanistan. The Afghansty were seeking post-war answers from Vietnam veterans. After all, their wars were similar, as were their experiences.

Through an arrangement by a global peace network out of Seattle, 19 Vietnam vets from all over the country flew to Alma Ata (now Almaty) in the republic of Kazakhstan, to meet with a contingent of battle-weary Russian warriors.

Having reported on vets over the years for KEYT-TV in Santa Barbara, I was asked to chronicle the exchange by University of California Santa Barbara professor Walter Capps, whose sterling class on the effects of the Vietnam War had gained national recognition.

Right from the outset, my videographer David Cronshaw and I ran into resistance from most of our traveling Vietnam vets who thought our presence would present a cinematic intrusion.

Another challenge arose once we touched down. Despite the dawning of Glasnost and Perestroika (Gorbachev's policies of political openness and economic restructuring), the Russian and American vets were initially skeptical of one another, mostly due to a staged and rigid gathering the first night, orchestrated by a flamboyant Russian film-maker whose roving camera lens and bright lights caught unassuming Americans off guard.

But after veterans from both countries got to know each other, tensions disappeared.

We Americans were billeted in a hotel normally occupied by the Russian Winter Olympics team, at the foot of the Tianshan mountain range bordering China.

Dave and I had little idea what to record at this point. But unbeknownst to us, our expedition in Alma Ata and later in Moscow would provide us with all the material we would need for the necessary images and a script.

We traveled to graveyards where mothers and fathers grieved over the loss of their sons. We visited churches where prayer was too late but solace was offered. We were invited to homes filled with joy or homes filled with emptiness. We photographed the portraits of young men who were killed in battle, boys who were told they would be building schools or constructing roads in a country where in reality war was waging between the "conquering" Soviet Union and Afghan freedom fighters, or Mujahideen.

The tombstones of the Russian dead and buried were not allowed to display how they died, or where. The sons of the Motherland were being deceived, as were their mothers and fathers.

We heard their stories and those of the Afghansty through Russian translators. One in particular, Olga Jouraleva, was seasoned in guiding foreign tourists in Moscow, a far cry from the role she now bravely accepted as an interpreter for the wounded.

And as good fortune would have it, an eloquent and compassionate Vietnam vet named Jack Lyon, a former Marine who saw action in the early part of the war, offered his perspective as a narrator for parts of our production. We were also lucky that none of our fragile equipment broke down in what was a very frozen and unfamiliar country.

On the flight home three weeks later one vet suggested we use a song from the rock group Dire Straights, "Brothers in Arms," as the theme and title of what would turn out to be an hour-long documentary. The haunting melody and melancholy lyrics worked out perfectly.

The Emmy-award winning documentary *Brothers in Arms* aired on KEYT (and eventually on PBS) in the latter days of February 1989, just as the Soviets were abandoning Afghanistan after a costly and futile struggle not unlike ours in Vietnam.

As the film reveals, no one understood this more that the veterans of those two conflicts who gathered and embraced for 10 emotional days in Alma Ata, halfway around the world, yet quite close to home.

[March 2008]

5

The News

I used to work for a guy who emotionally resembled Donald Trump. As a matter of fact, now that I think of it, I worked for a lot of guys like Donald Trump. I didn't realize it at the time, but when I entered the media business in 1976, I didn't know what power and insecurity could do to the soul. I should have known better.

~ *Newsbeat*

WENDY GRISSIM   BEN MORRISTON   KING HARRIS

KMST NEWSBEAT
weeknights at 6 & 11pm.
KMST 46
MONTEREY/SALINAS

On the Beach

Since this is my last week at KVEC, after nearly 10 years as news director, I thought I'd present to you my resume now that I'm "on the beach," meaning I'm in need of work.

Allow me to start at the beginning. I got my first radio gig in 1961 in the summertime when I worked for San Francisco powerhouse radio KSFO, where I helped the news department and gophered for popular morning radio genius Don Sherwood, who would urge his morning commute listeners to roll down their convertible tops, lower their windows, turn their radios up, and then he put on the sound of a siren. From San Jose to San Francisco, there was a 50-mile drone.

That was true radio, and I was hooked. So it was no surprise that as soon as I entered college, I got a job at the campus radio station as a disc jockey.

After I graduated, and having spent a year in Vietnam as an English teacher, I came home and went to a broadcasting school to get a first-class license to be able to go on the air, which I eventually did at an AM station in Vancouver, Washington.

That stint was interrupted when I joined a rock 'n' roll band in Los Angeles. When that journey ended after four years, I returned to radio in Monterey, hosting a midnight to 6 easy listening music program for 18 months on KWAV radio, which was in the same building as KMST, a local CBS television station that I joined as sports director in 1977—an eye-opening experience.

Soon I would be shooting video; about the same time I became news anchor and started to learn that the broadcast news media was not necessarily a kind one.

In 1980, after being demoted back to sports because of a change in ownership, I decided to look elsewhere. After a brief scuffle, I left for ABC affiliate KEYT in Santa Barbara, where I became news anchor and eventually news director for 17 years. During my tenure, we got hundreds of AP and UPI awards, and I received our first Emmy for a documentary I composed in late 1988 on Russian vets from Afghanistan meeting American vets from Vietnam.

By that time, lawyer Bob Smith had acquired KEYT, moving from Michigan to Santa Barbara so he could parade around with all the Hollywood types who lived in Montecito. In 1994, he fired general manager Sandy Benton, and replaced her with a not-so-honest fellow who thought he was a network executive, or the next coming. I knew my days were numbered.

Within a year, they hired a Kansas schoolmarm to take my job as news director, and they didn't renew my contract. I was out of there with little fanfare. But I soon hooked up with KSBY owner George Lilly, who asked if I could start up a Spanish speaking TV news show, which I did. My part in the project ended when I left Santa Barbara for a journalism lecturing position at Cal Poly in San Luis Obispo.

When that ended in three years, I got a news director position at KVEC, owned by a local insurance agent, who later sold it to Clear Channel, run by a guy who fired me for being too folksy.

KCOY had an opening for a producer at the time, so I took that and eventually became news director, a position that wasn't all that easy because the station had two couples, one working mornings, the other broadcasting evenings, and they loathed each other, even though they both resided a block apart on Harmony Lane in Orcutt, which I thought was pretty amusing.

Two years later, on the day of Michael Jackson's first Santa Maria court appearance, I was fired, for no reason really. Probably not corporate enough. I was still alive and kicking, and I landed an editorial management position at the alternative weekly New Times, while founder Steve Moss was in his waning days.

After he died, the manager of the joint accused me of leaking some news to the traditional press, which of course I did not do, so I gave him notice. A few months later, I got a job as a reporter with KVEC, owned by Clear Channel, until El Dorado bought the place a year later.

News director Ben Greenaway and I, making up the news staff, were terminated when El Dorado decided to cancel the morning news. The public outcry was stifling, prompting El Dorado to hire me back in 2007.

I would prefer to be with you in 2016, but that is not in the cards. I'm being terminated January 15, because of (I was told) budgetary constraints. So be aware if you have a desire to enter the news business, unless you like being on the beach.

But don't be afraid to enter the waters. Sometimes there are more sharks on land.

[January 2016]

Prompted by Profit

Having been a TV news anchor for 20 years, I had to chuckle when I spotted a recent Washington Post story that reported the anchors of one television station in the nation's capitol might soon be operating their own teleprompters.

This revelation did not surprise me in the least, because for years now owners and general managers, in their endless quest to cut the escalating and expensive operating costs of putting on a TV news broadcast, have been opting for computer-based systems that supposedly eliminate the need for costly personnel (like studio camera operators and floor directors) in favor of robotic cameras directed by coded information pre-programmed into the system by the producer of the newscast.

It's an ingenious concept, provided of course that the correct codes are added for each story; if not, you can expect a wild ride somewhere in the next 30 minutes.

Hurried and harried newscast producers and directors are bound to make mistakes. All it takes is one misplaced digit, and those mindless cameras take on a mind of their own. Picture errant pans or zooms, or incorrect and embarrassing shots of a very startled anchorman or anchorwoman, whose wide-eyed reaction, after suddenly realizing the red light above the camera into which they are staring is on, and it's on them, might reveal an expression that silently exclaims, "Hey! It's not my turn to read!" followed by an unscripted and not very well disguised expletive of some sort, usually in the form of a painful facial grimace of some kind.

Such is the price of progress, I suppose, but I somewhat feel sorry for news anchors already performing under such stressful and uncertain conditions who will now have to add another task to their nightly news functions—all to save money, of course.

According to the Post article, the station in question, WTTG, FOX Channel 5, "plans to reassign the technicians who operate the electronic prompters that feed scripted news copy to the anchors while they are on the air and have the anchors do it themselves by using a series of hand levers and foot pedals." Not like anchors don't have enough to do already.

Says one staffer, "Instead of orchestrating coverage, fact-checking, handling breaking news, paying attention to the newscast, engaging reporters, questioning authorities, covering bad writing and technical mistakes, anchors will now spend most of their time running the prompter."

In smaller markets, many stations already engage in this practice, where the anchor, or a tape editor, an unpaid intern, or for that matter anyone who is available, often runs the prompter, but for major-market larger stations with faster moving and whiz-bang complicated news shows, this may be a first.

I can already envision the latest new clause in the anchor contract: "You must operate your own teleprompter." I can as well envisage the response.

But as much as my heart goes out to all the well-paid anchors who may cringe at the idea, I'd like to point out they might be grateful. After all, at least they have teleprompters. When I got into the business in a small-market station in the 1970s, I had no such luxury. I memorized as much live copy as I could, ad-libbing into the camera, and waited until the film (yes, film—video wasn't prevalent yet) hopefully came up, which allowed me to look down and read the remainder of the script off camera.

I made do, but I can't say that for Dan Cullen, the guy who replaced me.

Dan was a much older and more "experienced" news anchor, a mustachioed Ted Baxter-type who took over my chair when the station changed ownership. When Dan realized that he'd never be getting a prompter from his new employers, he went out and bought a music stand, placed it right below the camera lens, and pleaded, begged or bribed any poor soul within range of the studio broadcast to turn the pages of a copy of his script settled on the stand's shelf.

This understandably presented more than a few challenges for my new colleague, not the least of which was that he still wasn't looking directly into the camera lens but below it, which fooled no one. Plus his contact lenses were always fogging up, mostly from the smoke of all the cigarettes he would inhale in the studio during the commercial breaks, making the already small print even more difficult to decipher, even if the script was turned to the correct page, which it often was not, either due to operator error, the breeze from the fans to cool the hot studio lights, or the complete collapse of the music stand itself.

I don't know where Dan is today, but I'd be willing to bet he might have been the guy who showed up at Channel 5, suitcase in hand, filled with all the hand levers and foot pedals a news operation needs for anchors to operate their own teleprompters.

And it wouldn't surprise me at all if his kit included that music stand.

[October 2009]

Give Me a Break

There are times when I miss TV news. Not the makeup or the camera, but the competition.

When I worked for KEYT in Santa Barbara, our rivals were KSBY in San Luis Obispo and KCOY in Santa Maria. That's because we're all in the same ratings market. It was kind of a dumb setup really, because nobody in San Luis or Santa Maria watched us and vice versa. But we competed nonetheless.

And boy was it fun.

Take for example 1985, when a rocket with an unknown payload was lifting off from Vandenberg Air Force Base and exploded. Actually, the Air Force caused the explosion on purpose because the launch was going to fail. The explosion left a huge brown cloud in the skies and it was headed for Lompoc.

Since we didn't have a bureau in north Santa Barbara County, I immediately sent a crew to the area in hopes we could get some kind of video. Meanwhile we were trying to reach Vandenberg, but their phone lines were busy being suddenly besieged by media from all over the place.

When I finally did get through to a public relations guy, his response to my questions was, "What cloud, sir?"

I informed my traveling crew that they would have to come up with some answers. Then I called the weather service and people there told me not to worry about the cloud or Lompoc, because whatever it was, it was headed out to sea. I told him thanks, and I usually don't worry about Lompoc anyway.

About an hour later, I got a call from my crew, and they said they had found some video from a resident who had taped the tail end of the disaster, but all it showed was a few puffs of smoke. Then I turned on KCOY and realized we had had it. They were showing a tease for their nightly news at 6:30, with pictures of the launch and the explosion. No way could we compete with that.

We were dismayed of course, because they now owned the story. But we weren't through yet. Knowing that KCOY with such great video would send it out to all their CBS affiliates, I figured that KCBS in Los Angeles would show it on their 5 o'clock newscast. So we taped it.

My co-anchor at the time, Kim Insley, looked at me and asked, "What are you doing?"

"I am calling KCBS to see if we can use part of that video."

"You'll never get it," she countered, "We are ABC."

"We've got nothing to lose," I said.

When the assignment desk answered my call, I asked whoever it was, "Hey, this is KEYT in Santa Barbara. Just saw your terrific video of the rocket explosion. Can we use part of it?"

"Who you with again?"

"KEYT."

"That's ABC, isn't it?"

"Yeah, but we gave you guys video of the Wheeler Fire in Ojai last year."

"Just a minute."

It was five minutes before he came back on the line. "Sure, go ahead and use all of it. Just don't give it to KABC."

Kim Insley rolled her eyes and walked away, as if prepared for my "Told you so." So at 6, we went on the air a half-hour before KCOY with their video. Gotcha!

They of course were livid. The next day I got a call from the top lawyer at CBS. "What's the idea of using our video?" he demanded from his lofty perch in the Black Rock in New York City.

"We got it from your station in Los Angeles."

"Well, who gave you permission to use it?"

"The assignment desk."

"Well, who was on the assignment desk?"

"I don't know; it's your station. You own and operate it."

"Listen you, if you ever show that video again you're gonna hear from us." But the cat was already out of the bag.

Later on that same year, we foiled KSBY. Then-Congressman Robert Lagomarsino had planned a helicopter trip from Santa Barbara to the Channel Islands to celebrate its National Park status. We knew KSBY had chartered a boat out of Ventura to record the occasion. I asked Lagomarsino's aid, a former KCOY reporter and cameraman, if we could send a photographer in the helicopter.

"Sorry, I can't, King, there's just no room." Then, the lightbulb.

"How about if we give you the camera and you take the pictures?"

"I don't think that will be a problem."

Of course, I knew that Congressman Lagomarsino would be in every shot, but I could live with that. While KSBY was still sailing the seas back to Ventura, we went on the air at 6 with our pictorial story. KSBY didn't broadcast their report until the next evening. Gotcha!

Kim Insley again shook her head. "King, you don't break a news story, you bend it."

[June 2010]

The Devil You Say

One of the most exasperating things in the news biz is trying to get a straight answer out of someone.

Sometimes all you get is a word, and even that doesn't quite cut it. Take, for example, a conversation I had with an Air Force official when I was reporting for KEYT-TV in Santa Barbara.

It occurred in April 1985, when a Titan rocket exploded after lifting off a launch pad from Vandenberg Air Force Base, sending out a brown cloud of mysterious gas over Lompoc. I was frantically making non-stop calls in an attempt to discern the danger of the cloud so we could warn the locals what to do.

Finally, after an hour, I got through.

"Sergeant, can you tell me what happened?"

"Yes, sir, we had an anomaly, sir."

"A what?"

"An anomaly, sir."

"By that, you mean a rocket blew up, right?"

"Yes, sir, it was an anomaly, sir."

"Did the rocket just explode or did you have to blow it up?"

"All I can tell you is that it was an anomaly, sir."

"Can you tell me about the gaseous cloud over Lompoc as a result of the explosion?"

"What cloud, sir?"

So I called the weather service, which told me not to worry, that the mysterious cloud, later determined noxious, was headed out to sea.

In all fairness, when any kind of accident or incident first occurs, it's sometimes difficult to assess what happened, certainly much less how or why. That comes later as the story unfolds.

But even then, information is (shall we say) handled with care, as exemplified by the latest fuss over an event that recently occurred at the Diablo Canyon Nuclear Power Plant, christened by PG&E as the Diablo Canyon Power Plant, a misnomer that hasn't fooled anybody over the years, from the protesters with the Abalone Alliance in the late '70s to the watchdogs at Mothers for Peace to this day.

And you can bet that when Mothers for Peace, like the rest of us, learned about a transformer fire at the facility on August 17, there were more questions than answers.

PG&E: "Unit reactor two remains shut down after a transformer failure caused a fire outside the plant's turbine building on Sunday at 12:12 a.m. We are investigating the cause and evaluating the scope of repairs, which will most likely include replacement of the transformer, and repairs to adjacent equipment in the yard including another transformer which was affected by debris associated with the fire which also caused some damage to the nearby administration building."

MFP: "The transformer fire was an explosive event that would have endangered workers if it had happened during the daytime, and it's fortunate workers weren't around or there would have been a lot of injuries."

PG&E: "We're calling it a fire because it was a fire. When a transformer catches on fire, there's a lot of oil in a transformer, and that makes for a very large fire which heats up, and we did have some debris from the fire that caused damage in the area. We're not calling it an explosion; we're calling it a transformer failure."

MFP: "It's not just a fire, it's a huge fire, and it's explosive. Oil is a great fire starter so once the thing ignites the oil, you've got an out-of-control, very violent, and explosive event happening. If you want to be accurate, you may call it a fire and an explosion, or explosive fire. PG&E uses the word fire, which is accurate, but it was more than that; it was an explosive event."

PG&E: "The electrical fault occurred in a high-voltage bushing. That bushing failed, causing the outer ceramic surface to disintegrate and the insulating oil to burn and scorch the outside of the transformer. We did have some other damage like some broken windows in the administration building. We're putting protective film on those windows that prevents penetration through glass, and erecting some protective walls around other transformers. We have also restricted the area to essential personnel only. It's certainly a lesson learned. We realize we were very fortunate that this happened on a weekend night when we didn't have a lot of personnel there. There certainly would have been a higher risk of injury had it been a normal work day, so we have taken additional steps to improve personal safety to minimize that risk, in the unlikely event that such a thing happens again."

PG&E had to add, of course, that there was no release of radioactive material to the environment from the event because despite what the sign says, it is after all a nuclear power plant.

But I'm still unsure if the event was a fire or an explosion, or a fire that caused an explosion, or an explosion that caused a fire, an explosive fire, or an explosive event.

I'd favor the latter except I will offer something simpler: How about an anomaly?

[September 2008]

Brothers in Broadcasting

I find it rather amusing (if not curious) in following NBC's recent late night comedy of errors, that in this era of viewer independence, there still exists corporate demigods who believe their dictate and significance infallible.

Having once been a member of the ABC-TV affiliate advisory board, which included trips to its headquarters in New York City, I have had business with many of this ilk, most of them who, in aspiring to the highest echelons of power, take their positions so imperiously.

"Kind of arrogant, aren't they?" the sterling news anchor Peter Jennings once remarked to me, referring to network brass, after I told him about my trials with his bosses over a documentary I had produced for ABC affiliate KEYT-TV in Santa Barbara.

I had traveled with my cameraman Dave Cronshaw to the hinterlands of Mother Russia in late 1988 to record a rare meeting between Vietnam veterans and Soviet soldiers who had recently returned from their own quagmire in Afghanistan and needed support in coping with the cruel consequence of such a similar futile war.

During our three-week journey, which took us to Moscow and then over to Almaty in the republic of Kazakhstan, Dave captured incredible pictures and stunning scenes of places and events where no American videographers up to that time had ever been allowed to go. We trekked to churches and cemeteries, memorials and museums, hospitals and homes. Mostly we met with wounded war veterans forever scarred by their experience, and despondent mothers and fathers forever scarred by the unfathomable loss of their sons.

On the flight home, I decided to use as a theme and title for our story the musical anti-military masterpiece "Brothers in Arms," written by Mark Knopfler of Dire Straits, who would give me permission to use it.

After logging all the extraordinary footage we had, I was certain that ABC News would be interested, because for one thing nobody else had anything like it, and for another it was very timely—in two months, Russia would be pulling out of Afghanistan. I thought our stories revealed why.

So I called all the major ABC news programs at the time: 20/20, Good Morning America, Nightline, and World News Tonight, all of whom said they weren't interested.

I called Robert Murphy in charge of ABC News coverage, and asked him how he could turn down such valuable video sight unseen (corporate mindset at the time being that small market TV stations couldn't possibly shoot anything up to network standards). Murphy reluctantly acquiesced and sent down San Francisco Bureau Chief Lynn Jones, who after seeing our video wrote Murphy: "It would be hard to beat what KEYT has, even if we did the story ourselves the next time a group of Americans go."

I never heard back from Murphy, but I did get wind that 20/20, the first outfit that rejected us, was sending a crew over to Moscow to replicate what we had done.

That didn't concern me greatly; I believed their 20-minute segment to be aired before ours would be forced, staged, and impersonal. What bothered me was that they had blatantly misappropriated the title *Brothers in Arms*. Understandably alarmed, I alerted ABC News Chief Roone Arledge and insisted 20/20 change the name of their report, which was done at the last minute.

But I'd had enough. Not long after KEYT aired *Brothers* in late February of 1989, I attended ABC's annual meeting of affiliate general managers in Los Angeles with the sole purpose of presenting their top dogs with my low opinion.

"Now," announced Tom Murphy, CEO of Cap Cities/ABC, from a

dais crowded with his fellow executive colleagues, "As you know, we pride ourselves on our great working relationship with our esteemed affiliates. Before we all leave to mingle with all the stars in Hollywood, are there any comments, questions, concerns, or complaints? We'd like to hear them, any or all."

"Mr. Murphy," I spoke up with microphone in hand, feeling not unlike a student standing on his desktop in *Dead Poets Society*, armed and ready to challenge the powers that be. "I have a big problem with ABC News."

Amidst a vast sea of now suddenly intrigued but restless broadcasters, which included, unbeknownst to me, Bob Smith, the owner of KEYT standing in back of the hall, and Sandy Benton, my general manager sitting next to me now trying desperately to hide under her chair, I began to state my case for justice.

I believe it was right after my use of the word hypocrisy that Murphy cut short my blistering oratory, advising me even though he asked for it that this was not the proper forum for such conduct, and directing me to register my grievances to my affiliate advisor, who not surprisingly arranged to have me voted off his board.

Brothers was picked up by PBS and went on to win an array of prestigious awards, including an Emmy. What tickled me just as much is when Bob Smith turned to Sandy Benton at the end of ABC's convention and asked, "King's not coming back here next year, is he?"

[January 2010]

Action News

I was saddened to hear about the passing of Frank Magid the other day. Magid, a gentleman in the truest sense of the word, was considered the world's top television news and programming consultant, the man responsible for the creation of the "Action News" format delivered by happy talk anchors.

The highly professional and polished Magid (rhymes with "ragged"), who had to have been born a statistician, formed an audience research company called Frank N. Magid Associates in Cedar Rapids, Iowa in the late 1950s. His firm's modus operandi was (and still is) to survey your audience and then advise you on the changes needed to increase your ratings (for more than a nominal fee, of course).

Included in the package was a news consultant along with a talent coach. I got to know Frank quite well through my work as news director and anchor for KEYT-TV in Santa Barbara during the '80s and '90s, when we were one of his clients.

Now I can't honestly say I was overjoyed when I first learned midway through my career that I'd be working with an outfit as prestigious as Magid Associates; mentioning the word "consultant" to a news director sometimes initiates a reaction not unlike that of a Vietnam veteran who cringes every time the name "Jane Fonda" is invoked. Nobody likes to be informed their product might be inferior.

Why, I'd ask of my general manager, do we need to spend a lot of money we don't have on a consultant when we all know that geography dictates the perennial ratings winner in our market? It's not like all three competing television stations (KEYT, KSBY, and KCOY) operate in the same city.

"Because," she would say, "There's always room for improvement." Which, translated, really meant, "We have no choice because that's what Bob wants." Bob was Bob Smith, the impetuous owner of KEYT at the time. Enough said, argument over, case closed.

It was no secret that Smith chose Magid not only because of the status, but to keep our competitors from hiring him. Given the mechanics of our marketplace, which included San Luis Obispo County to the north and all of Ventura County to the south, I remained somewhat skeptical about any drastic changes in the ratings structure.

Normally, when a station hires Magid Associates, it doesn't engage the man himself, just some handpicked members from his Cedar Rapids staff of 300 or so. The Magid consultant, more often than not a former TV news director, reviews tapes of your news shows and critiques them for content, style, presentation, and production. The Magid talent coach works with anchors addressing such marketable issues as delivery, credibility, sincerity, and, of course, dress.

Keep in mind when dealing with smaller market TV stations, youth and inexperience exposes you to all kinds of challenges, lest you be fortunate enough to land a big fish from a major market who has tired of the Tinsel-town turmoil, and even then you're not out of the woods.

In my case, Frank Magid left Cedar Rapids and moved to Santa Barbara in the early '90s, so he himself would get involved in his consulting process. To no one's surprise, especially mine, he would often call me up after viewing one of our nightly news broadcasts and offer various observations.

"King."

"Yes, Frank."

"Do you know that every time your co-anchor Debby Davison looks at you, she purses her lips?"

"I was unaware of that, Frank, and I'm curious as to what that means, but I appreciate your notice and will pass it on to the talent coach."

Frank didn't miss a trick.

"King."

"Good evening, Frank."

"I think it's a great idea that your Ventura County reporter Larry Good produces several stories from his beat as opposed to only one major package...makes it seem like we're all over the place down there."

"Thanks, Frank. Good suggestion." And it was.

He could also be quite stern when things did not go well.

"King."

"Hello, Frank."

"Where was your video on that breaking story at the top of the news?"

"Well, Frank, we have an intern loading the tape machines, and he screwed up. All we can afford."

His deafening silence led me to believe that he wasn't so much interested in my budgetary problems as he was in just finding a solution to the situation.

Sometimes his recommendations were, I thought, downright dangerous. One night he called and informed me that after extensive Magid research, it was revealed, for credibility purposes, that the male anchor best be seated on the right side of the set, the position that my strong-willed, equal rights colleague Debby Davison currently occupied.

"King."

"Hi, Frank."

"I think you should switch chairs with Debby so that she is to your left."

"Frank, if you want to be the one to tell Debby Davison where and why she should sit to my left, please be my guest, but if you do, you might consider wearing a flak jacket."

That got a chuckle. "I'll take it under advisement, King."

"Well, Frank," I replied, "it was you who wanted action news."

[February 2010]

Power of the Press

By the time you read this, I have little doubt that more harm will have come to the courageous local and international journalists who have been risking their lives and their safety to the chaotic events unfolding in Egypt.

Just after the defiant President Hosni Mubarak stated that he would not relinquish his power until his term expired towards the end of this year, all hell broke loose in Tahrir Square in Cairo when pro-Mubarak forces (including secret police) violently clashed with protesters of the Mubarak regime, who had for the most part gathered peacefully up until that time.

Caught up in this attack were journalists attempting to get the word out on what was going on.

Reporters and videographers were forcibly detained, arrested with no cause, shot, stabbed, and beaten. With the Internet already having been shut down by the government, many felt that this latest round of suppression was purposely orchestrated by Mubarak loyalists and thugs.

So far, as of this writing, at least one reporter has been killed. Ahmed Mohammed Mahmoud, who worked for the state-run newspaper Al-Ahram, was taking pictures of fighting between security forces and protesters from the balcony of his home adjacent to Tahrir Square when he was shot January 28. The 36-year-old Egyptian journalist died of his wounds a week later.

During the week leading up to his death, one report out of Cairo claimed Mubarak supporters assaulted dozens of correspondents with virtual impunity and little intervention from nearby military units.

A Swedish TV reporter was hospitalized after being stabbed in the back. A CBS news crew was jailed for a day. CNN's Anderson Cooper and his camerawoman were physically assaulted. The next day the car in which they were riding was violently attacked, forcing both to flee from the danger in the square to the relative safety of an obscure dimly-lit hotel room. One NBC producer was threatened when he was told he would be beheaded. And officials from the Qatar-based Al-Jazeera television network, whose coverage (despite efforts to black it out) provided indispensable pictures with storylines, said their offices in Cairo and all equipment inside were set ablaze and destroyed.

The United Nations said the brazen assaults on reporters were an attempt to stifle coverage, President Obama said the attacks were "unacceptable," and White House press secretary Robert Gibbs said he was disturbed by reports of journalists being systematically targeted.

In response, the Egyptian government said reports of an official policy against international media were false. The state-run Cairo Press Center, which has issued press credentials to more than a thousand reporters, could only respond: "Regrettably, international journalists have been endangered by the same conditions that have threatened all Egyptians in areas of the country where there have been major disturbances and a breakdown of security."

Having lived in or reported from countries corrupt or those ruled by dictators or puppets, it's been my experience that if you decide to enter the fray, you're taking grave chances.

During my year-long tour in Vietnam, I viewed the arrests of several American and South Vietnamese reporters by the "White Mice" (Saigon police) who did not appreciate their corrupt activities being exposed.

The reporters were always freed provided, of course, they paid a ridiculous fee.

When I traveled to the Soviet Union in 1988 to record a meeting between American Vietnam veterans and Russian soldiers having just returned from Afghanistan, my cameraman Dave Cronshaw and I were hounded every step of the way. Despite this being the Gorbachev era of Glasnost (openness) and Perestroika (political and economic restructuring), the Soviet government, military, and particularly the infamous spy network KGB did not trust and barely tolerated our presence or our intentions.

We of course in turn did not trust anyone Russian. Our biggest liability was that neither Dave nor I spoke their language, so we depended heavily on two translators who traveled with our group. Thank God they were there, because every time we set up to shoot in Moscow's Red Square, we were ordered by a small army of ultra-paranoid soldiers (who surrounded us everywhere we went) with machine guns aimed at our heads to immediately stop. Or else.

In Kazakhstan, where we were to meet our war veteran counterparts, a Russian film director desiring to film the exchange as well had staged the initial encounter with bright lights and cameras rolling intent on capturing background information on every U.S. vet there, while not providing or demanding the same from the Soviet soldiers in attendance.

Sensing the unease, Dave and I, and our entire entourage for that matter, thought it was a setup. Only when the vets opened up to one another did the purpose of our visit become a reality, despite the lurking presence of two KGB agents posing as travel agent and tour guide, who we referred to as Boris and Natasha.

Words of advice to aspiring foreign correspondents: Don't let danger dissuade you from your duty. Freedom is worth fighting for, even if your weapon is just that of a camera, phone, or laptop. Or passion or desire.

I'm certain that the family of Ahmed Mohammed Mahmoud, for one, would appreciate it.

[February 2011]

Televisionaries

Here I was, out of work. After nearly 20 years with KEYT-TV in Santa Barbara, I was shown the door, but given the people who were running the place in early 1997, I wasn't all that unhappy about it.

I was soon ecstatic when I was given the opportunity to build and organize what I thought had always been desperately needed for the market, and that was a Spanish-speaking television news operation.

The audience for such a venture was there. Hispanics made up 42 percent of the local population and I had witnessed modest success with KEYT's Spanish simulcast of our 5 o'clock news, which was first introduced in 1989 by general manager Sandy Benton.

While the Latino community appreciated the gesture, I had realized that interpreting our news had its limitations. One person who passionately agreed with that was the translator himself, my good friend Ruben Keoseyan, who on more than one occasion had talked with me about the need to go beyond a simulcast and create a Spanish language program that offered news and information aimed directly towards Hispanics.

While both of us shared the vision, neither one of us had the means, until KSBY-TV San Luis Obispo and Cox Cable of Santa Barbara came into the picture. Asked if I would start up and manage a Hispanic TV news endeavor, I agreed without hesitation, knowing I had Ruben in my back pocket.

Nonetheless, both of us realized resources would be limited and the enterprise challenging. KSBY supplied the equipment, Cox provided the studio, and Ruben became the anchor for a show we decided to call *Notidiario*, for daily news.

"I had a little TV experience in Mexico," he recently told me, "And then you threw me on live during KEYT's coverage of the Painted Cave fire to translate the disaster for the Latino community. I felt I could do anything after that experience."

Ruben and I then set out to hire the rest of the staff, which would need training in reporting, photography, and editing.

Alex Transilito, whose girlfriend worked for Cox, was our sports guy. For weather we found a talented woman named Blanca Figueroa, who also loaded the tapes during the newscast. I discovered Andres Angulo while I was visiting the Mexican Consulate in Oxnard. He was dating the Consulate's daughter. Andres became our star reporter.

"What was amazing, King," Ruben said, "Is that all these people, who were willing like ourselves to work for peanuts, had very little experience when they started out. You trained everybody."

Be that as it may, Ruben and I collaborated on just about every other task, like spending our weekends staining a primitive news desk and exterior background set that was fashioned together by a carpenter who owed me a favor, and setting up and sometimes blindly arranging as much illumination as we could to bring as much light to our anchor team as well as our project.

KSBY engineered a portable cart that housed a mini control panel, a couple of playback tape machines, and an elementary graphics computer used to produce the newscast, plus the necessary VHS camera equipment needed for capturing the news in the field and in the studio.

With the official airdate scheduled for the beginning of June, all of us had less than a month to organize how to shoot, log, write, and edit news stories to be delivered on air by Ruben.

We knew our production initially wouldn't be slick, but that didn't matter. "The Latino community appreciated news catered for them," according to Ruben. "That never happened before. They could do away with quality as long as the information was useful and that's what we focused on. We stayed away from fanciness of the news, the colors, the graphics, and focused on giving people information, which is the core of news. We presented news they could use, news that was relevant."

Notidiario debuted at the beginning of summer. We recorded it weeknights at 6, and Cox broadcast it at 7.

When I left in September to teach journalism at Cal Poly, Ruben took over the reins. "We took a few steps back losing your technical advice, but during the next few years *Notidiario* gained acceptance that was incredible.

"However, since we couldn't expand our coverage to Santa Maria, the operation got just too expensive. I'm proud to say that Univision eventually assimilated *Notidiario*, taking over the core of the newscast that you and I started."

At the end of a successful reign at *Notidiario*, Ruben worked for prominent Latino newspapers in Los Angeles and Puerto Rico, and today publishes La Raza newspaper out of Chicago.

"We were visionaries, King," he said. "*Notidiario* was a preamble, if you will. We knew there was a need there, and we were willing to work for practically nothing to get it done. It was great fun. I remember telling you when it was a dream that someday it's going to happen, and it might as well be us."

I'm grateful that it was.

[May 2010]

Pomp and Circumstance

When I was hired to teach journalism at Cal Poly as a full-time lecturer in 1997, little did I know that part of the job would include attending the winter and spring graduation ceremonies in required regalia of cap and gown, a traditional outfit that eluded me when I departed college, because in 1968 assassinations, riots, and tear gas were in vogue, which encouraged many a student (and professor I might add) to fashion a more appropriate attire (like gas mask or flak jacket).

I'd like to say I avoided my sendoff to the "real world" because of that reason alone, but I had changed my major to English late in the game and that caused me to take summer classes in order to graduate. Any pomp and circumstance that I missed as an undergraduate I would gratefully find myself taking part in many years later as a teacher at a prestigious university.

Of course, like the students I taught, I had to earn that honor as well, which wasn't all that easy considering more than a few, sadly enough, lacked the basic skills in grammar necessary to write a simple news narrative.

I knew I was in for a long semester whenever I heard a question like "What's a comma?"

It was at this point that I decided to add a lengthy lesson in sentence structure to all the structured courses I was teaching at the time, which included radio and television news production and announcing, and writing for print and broadcast news, two totally disparate styles of communication which at times led to understandably predictable and natural confusion on the part of some students taking both classes.

"Why do you spell out 'dollar' for broadcast and use the '$' sign for print?"

When other students answered, "Because 'dollar' is easier for broadcasters to read," I not only knew I was making progress, but the directions the individual students were taking as well: those who favored the "$" sign eventually went on to work for The Mustang Daily, Cal Poly's newspaper, and those who preferred "dollar" made their way to KCPR radio or CPTV television, the two campus broadcasting outlets.

I was hoping that by the time they got to wherever they were going, they would have embraced the responsibility, objectivity, and common sense that should be intrinsic in all good reporters. If there was any weakness in the program, it was in the overpriced books students were forced to pay for, outdated texts offering phrases of a by-gone era.

A suggestion from one, for example, was to avoid using clichés like "the cat's pajamas." Mention that to a 20-year-old in today's world and a response like "What?" shouldn't surprise you.

Consequently, a suggestion from me was to return the books, get out of the classroom, and embrace the Cal Poly motto "learn by doing."

How about a trip to the courtroom, where a man is being sentenced for murder? Or a visit to the de Groot Nursing Home for medically-fragile children? Or a stopover at the SLO County Board of Supervisors meeting? Students who wrote reports after experiencing such venues told me they learned more from those engagements than practically anything passed before them in a classroom or laboratory.

I am happy and proud to say that many of the bright students I was lucky enough to teach over an incredible three-year period at Cal Poly are leading very successful careers in print and broadcasting, here on the Central Coast and points well beyond.

I was also pleased and honored to see them all decked out in cap and gown before we went our separate ways. I vividly recall the march down to Mustang Stadium, where the euphoria rivaled the sunshine and the enthusiasm equaled the expectations, save for one obsessively self-controlled dean's assistant whose role she decided was to instruct us all to proceed in an orderly procession of two-by-two, a futile command that much to her frustrated dismay failed to work because the last thing on the mind of any prospective grad at this moment in life is submission to any kind of ridiculous authority.

Delirious students who could barely contain themselves charged out onto the field, scrambling for their assigned chairs just so they could mount them to search for their parents and loved ones elusively buried somewhere in the stands.

Here before me were hundreds of kids, darting like chipmunks popping up out of their holes, all dressed in black, pirouetting on their portable chairs, waving wildly with one hand, holding a cell phone with the other, trying to track down the location of moms and dads, all of whom were exhibiting the same frantic behavior. If I heard a shriek above the din, which occurred more than I thought possible, I knew someone had connected.

The ceremony that followed was overshadowed by the growing anticipation of the celebration to follow, where hats would sail, dreams would soar, and tears would flow amidst hugs embracing the future as well as the past, but mostly the present.

No need to declare "I made it through!"—radiant smiles all around said it all. It was pomp and circumstance at its best, well worth the price of a cap and gown and all my attempts to explain that confounded comma.

[June 2010]

Newsbeat

I used to work for a guy who emotionally resembled Donald Trump. As a matter of fact, now that I think of it, I worked for a lot of guys like Donald Trump.

I didn't realize it at the time, but when I entered the media business in 1976, I didn't know what power and insecurity could do to the soul. I should have known better. Especially after having seen the Humphrey Bogart flick *Deadline USA* when I was a kid.

It's a movie about life in the news business, in this case the death of a newspaper. Bogart is managing editor of a widely respected and daring major metropolitan newspaper that valiantly exposes the city's crime czar only to be bought out and shut down by a weakly-regarded competitor.

Not much dramatic license was needed here, sad to say, for the reality is that ownership of journalistic enterprises has been changing hands over the years with alarming alacrity, as I have discovered more than once in my 30-year career as a newsman.

Not long after I first started anchoring and reporting news in 1977 for KMST in Monterey, the locally owned station was sold to Retlaw Broadcasting (that's the Walt Disney family–Retlaw is Walter spelled backwards), which owned television outfits in the Central Valley.

Retlaw made immediate alterations, like bringing in a Will Ferrell-type A-N-C-H-O-R-M-A-N, changing the program name to "The News" (only effective if you say it from a mountaintop), and relegating yours truly to sports. So I decided to leave.

But it was during a ratings period (which never made any difference because rival station KSBW was the perennial powerhouse in our market). That prompted the never-been-a-general-manager-before to demand that I return my fitted wardrobe, which I didn't because who else could wear my fitted jackets and slacks?

From that point on, the "Harris clause" took effect: "Due to the stupidity and naiveness of a former employee, all clothes will be treated as company property like typewriters, computers, and furniture."

So in May of 1980 my wife Sara and I and our golden retriever Huntley moved to Santa Barbara, where I anchored and reported KEY News at KEYT, which was owned by a local rancher.

Guess what happened next? A few years after I got there, he sold the fabled hilltop station to Shamrock Broadcasting (the Roy Disney family—and no, I'm not making this up).

Guess what happened next? Roy, when presented with an offer he couldn't refuse two years later, sold it to a Rupert Murdock wannabe from Michigan who wanted to hang with the Hollywood crowd in Montecito. That pretty much signaled the end of my 16-year stint as anchor and 10-year tenure as news director at KEYT. Since "Rupert" and his wunderkind GM demanded the spotlight, suffice it to say my contract wasn't renewed.

I then took a respite from broadcasting and moved to San Luis Obispo with an opportunity to teach journalism at Cal Poly for two years. But I delved back into the business as news director and anchor at KVEC radio in 1999.

Guess what happened next? Clear Channel bought the news-talk AM station less than two years later and hired a new manager, so I went back to television as producer and eventually director of the news team at KCOY in Santa Maria.

Guess what happened next? Clear Channel bought KCOY, whose GM two years later told me he was moving in a different direction and it wasn't mine, so I found myself (as so many others in this business do) "on the beach," an industry expression which has nothing to do with frolicking along the seashore.

My sojourn didn't last long, fortunately, when I was hired by the New Times newspaper to be managing editor.

Guess what happened next? The highly spirited owner of the feisty tabloid suddenly died, which ultimately resulted in the sale of the alternative weekly and my eventual resignation. Not long after, in September of last year, I returned to KVEC.

Guess what happened next? Clear Channel announced it was selling many of its radio entities, including the cluster of eight stations it operates on the Central Coast. El Dorado Broaddcasting bought the operation and held it for 10 years.

Guess what happened next? KVEC was sold and I lost my job.

Now you might conclude that with all these changes I might be cursed. I don't think I am. Almost everyone I know in the news biz has been on the beach at one time or another. Still, it would be nice to be able to do your job without having to look over your shoulder all the time.

I may be somewhat retired, but why do I get the feeling my days with Donald aren't over?

[February 2017]

6

Music

Hey, I didn't carry no switchblades; I just like music with a beat to it. So rock that around your clock. And when Elvis hit the scene I screamed as loud as all those 16-year-old girls because I knew that rock 'n' roll was here to stay.

- Deal with the Devil

Deal with the Devil

April 19 is Record Store Day, in honor of all the independent retail stores like Boo Boo Records in San Luis Obispo that still sell vinyl LPs and 45s.

It's a day near and dear to my heart, because the only way you heard music back in the 1950s and '60s was by placing a 12-inch or seven-inch recording on a turntable and letting her rip. While 78 RPM records were still available, they were being phased out by vinyl that could handle more songs and wouldn't break if they were dropped.

Columbia and RCA were the chief competitors in this new marketplace in the late 1940s. Columbia invented the Long Play initially for classical music, and RCA engineered the seven-inch single with a big hole in it for the pop market. RCA could afford to take such a chance; the company made special record players to play the smaller discs.

My parents bought me one such machine, and it was one of the worst decisions they ever made. You see, prior to that time, the music source in a post-fifties home was in the form of a big console in the living room, where everyone gathered to listen to what the grown-ups wanted to hear, like musicals, classical, and pop. Now with my new portable machine, with tiny speaker included, I could bug out of that scene, which I did, and stay in my room all day rocking and rolling to Little Richard *et al.*

Of course, no one in our household ever saw me again, and everybody shook their heads whenever they walked by my room where my walls lost their plaster from sounds like "Tutti Frutti" and "Whole Lotta Shakin' Going On."

From that point on, as they used to say in the parlance of the day, I was a real gone cat, which meant that since I avoided classical, jazz, tin pan alley, or folk and preferred music written by "cretinous goons" (as Frank Sinatra once said), I was labeled like everyone else in my blue suede shoes as a juvenile delinquent.

Hey, I didn't carry no switchblades; I just liked music with a beat to it. So rock that around your clock. And when Elvis hit the scene, I screamed as loud as all those 16-year-old girls because I knew that rock 'n' roll was here to stay.

I also knew that I had to work in order to buy all those 45s I wanted to listen to. That's when I met Joe Prein, who owned a record store on Santa Cruz Avenue in Menlo Park. The neatest thing about his store were the three or four booths lined up along the wall, where you could enter a private domain and listen to records on machines constructed for such a purpose. You didn't even have to buy them. But of course I did. With interest.

"You want to buy that? It'll cost you 89 cents," he demanded.

"I haven't got 89 cents, I'm a kid," I replied. "How 'bout a quarter for a down payment?"

"I'll do you one better," he said. "Since you've been in here every day for the last two weeks and wore out all my needles on my record machines, I see the value of you as a potential customer. So I am going to set you up with a charge account. You know what that is?" I was nine. My idea of a big time was a candy bar. My eyes wandered over to all the platters he hung up on his walls.

"No, sir," I answered, but I knew a deal was about to be made.

"You can have this record today, and you don't have to pay for it until next week."

"What's the catch?" I queried. Even at my age I was dumb but not stupid.

"A penny per record interest," said Joe Prein, who knew he could now make a living off of just me alone.

"Wow!" I exclaimed.

"All you have to do is sign right here," he prompted, with a twinkle in his eye. I scribed my signature, and signed my life away. I was broke for a long time and suffered the summertime blues.

But I felt like a rich man, thanks to old Joe Prein. He gave me the opportunity to enjoy the music on vinyl I still love to this day. Hi-fi or stereo, he was one hell of a record store guy.

[April 2014]

Yesterday

February. 1963. Fifty years ago. I was motoring along El Camino Real in Redwood City in my '46 Ford Coupe tuned into one of five rock 'n' roll radio stations I had programmed.

I heard this musical sound I'd never experienced before. The production of the selection sounded somewhat sparse compared to most of the orchestrated pop music of the day, but very lively and upbeat, and quite unusual. The record being played certainly caught my attention.

The radio in my Ford was nothing to rave about, but it beat any one of the transistors that were glued to my ear as I was growing up. I was addicted to the Top Forty, long before Elvis made the scene. So I loved all kinds of music, especially when something new and different hit the charts, like the song I was listening to now.

I remember the DJ coming along after the record was over, announced by a fury of drum fills: "You heard it first on KYA. That was 'Please Please Me' by a group from England called the Beatles."

Of course as a listener, I couldn't discern the spelling, so I thought he meant Beetles. That's an odd name for a group, I thought to myself, even though a few years before, Buddy Holly's group the Crickets had become an accepted hit parade moniker. There were other groups like the Spiders, Butterflies, and Fireflies who sported names of insects, so I guess I shouldn't have been surprised. When I found out "Beetles" was actually "Beatles," I thought that was very clever.

Keep in mind, although I didn't know it then, the Beatles at this time had become very popular in Europe, and wouldn't break out in the U.S. till the end of 1963. They had tried as early as April 1962 with

"My Bonnie," which fell on deaf ears. So did three other Beatles tunes released here in 1963, including "Please Please Me," "From Me To You," and "She Loves You." No wonder. Record store owners didn't carry them; they didn't know who the Beatles were.

All this would change in December, just days after the Kennedy assassination, when the U.S. and the rest of the world were treated to "I Want To Hold Your Hand," released just prior to their first television appearance on the Ed Sullivan Show the following February 9.

On that Sunday night, I, like everybody else, was sitting two feet away from my TV set straining to see and experience what kind of group could make all this commotion, one similar to that of Elvis the pelvis eight years earlier. As I sat there mesmerized, jumping around to "All My Loving," I thought, So this is the group that I first heard a year ago. Great music, incredible energy, terrific personalities, but what's with the hair?

As I continued to watch, totally captivated, my senses zeroed in on Ringo, for he (like me) was a drummer—but no ordinary drummer. I was to find out later that one of the things that made Ringo so outstanding, other than his relentless backbeat and his curious use of hi-hat cymbals, was that he was left-handed but playing right-handed, which made his fills so unusual.

Another story has it that when Ringo was hired to replace drummer Pete Best, the Beatles' producer, George Martin, initially thought he was lousy, and even had him sit out on their first record "Love Me Do," which he did, playing a tambourine instead. Due to pressure from the group, Martin recorded another version with Ringo playing the traps.

Ultimately, and this I've always found amusing considering Martin's first impression of Mr. Starr, Ringo turned out to be the quintessential musician of the group, rarely if at all making a mistake during their recording career in the studio.

One other admirer of Ringo I should mention. Not long after the Beatles' arrival, the record industry started recognizing their popularity. One song in particular was released, called "Ringo I Love You," a collector's dream because it's very rare. It was produced by Phil Spector and recorded by one Cherilyn Sarkesian LaPiere under the name of Bonnie Jo Mason. It didn't chart, but it was Cher's very first recording.

By the time the Beatles' February tour (including two more appearances on the Sullivan show) was coming to a close, the first song I ever heard them sing and play, "Please Please Me," and all the others I had missed, were dominating the Top Ten of the pop charts, and would for months and years to come.

I never saw the Beatles in person, even though they opened and closed their live performances over the years in my home town of San Francisco: too much screaming, hysteria, and jellybeans.

But on that one day in February of 1963, I heard what was to come, and although I didn't know it at the time, it sure changed my tune.

[January 2013]

The Magical Mystery Chord

I can't believe it's been 50 years since the Beatles first struck a chord in America and the world beyond, and 50 years ago this week right smack dab in mid-summer of 1964 that they struck THE chord.

I'm referring to those mysterious notes that were played to introduce their number one hit single, "A Hard Day's Night," which also reverberated in their debut movie of the same name.

While to this day no one seems to know the identity of THE chord, a lot of musically-minded folks have offered up various opinions, like the following from a blogger named Patrick, whose view along with thousands of others can be found at *www.beatlesbible.com*: ". . . my guess is that the musicians really didn't care what the name of the chord was, perhaps they didn't even know . . . there is no doubt that it is a Dm7add11."

Hey Patrick, Beatle George Harrison says it was a Fadd9.

Whatever.

While we may not know exactly the name of THE opening chord, we do know the instruments that were used to play it: most notably George on a Rickenbacker-360 12-string guitar, John on a Gibson J-160 six-string acoustic guitar, Paul on a Hofner violin bass, Ringo on cymbals and snare drum, and producer George Martin on a Steinway grand piano.

Says Martin about THE chord: "We knew it would open both the film and the soundtrack LP, so we wanted a particularly strong and effective beginning. The strident guitar chord was the perfect launch."

THE chord was instantly recognizable. Similar notes were used for a fade at the end of the record.

The album, by the way, was the first Beatles LP to feature all tracks written by McCartney and Lennon.

While "A Hard Day's Night" sat on top of Billboard's Hot 100 list for the first week of August, five other songs from the album were on the charts as well: "I'll Cry Instead," "And I Love Her," "If I Fell," "I'm Happy Just To Dance With You," and "I Should Have Known Better."

The non-Lennon-McCartney composition "Ain't She Sweet" also made the charts in the same period. While the Fab Four had been extremely successful owning the Top 100 up to this point (they had the top five records on the charts in April), other artists from Britain and America were well represented.

On August 1, the first wave of the British Invasion included the likes of Dusty Springfield, the Swinging Blue Jeans, Lulu and the Lovers, Mille Small, Gerry and the Pacemakers, the Searchers, Cilla Black, Billy J. Kramer, and the Dakotas singing a Beatles song, as did Peter and Gordon, the Dave Clark Five, and the Rolling Stones. John and Paul wrote so many great pop songs they could and did give them away.

Even the Boston Pops Orchestra legitimized the Beatles with its rendition of "I Want to Hold Your Hand," much to the shock of parents who couldn't figure out what was going on with this frenzied musical atmosphere presenting us with all these longhairs playing rock 'n' roll!

Speaking of rock 'n' roll, first generation rockers like Chuck Berry, Little Richard, Sam Cooke, and Elvis were on this same chart, as were girl groups like the Dixie Cups, whose "Chapel of Love" went to number one, and the Supremes, who were about to, with "Where Did Our Love Go?" to be followed by several consecutive number ones.

Representing doo-wop, the Four Seasons had just topped the charts with "Rag Doll" and the Drifters produced "Under the Boardwalk." The Beach Boys and Jan and Dean led the hot rod race.

Motown and soul music were on the rise, and even crooners like Dean Martin would enter number one amidst all this, which is no surprise really when you consider that jazz great Louis Armstrong had a top hit with "Hello Dolly" at the peak of the British Invasion.

But of all the summer sounds I heard 50 years ago this August, while cruising around in my '56 Chevy, none struck home like THE chord.

I doubt I'll hear the likes of it again.

[July 2014]

The Last Waltz

Anyone who knows me a little bit will realize pretty early on that I grew up as a rock 'n' roller with a transistor radio glued to my ear so I wouldn't miss the latest hits spewing forth.

Radio was the only way I could tune in to this music with a beat, since the only record player in the house was an RCA console in the living room firmly under my parent's control, which meant for the most part all we got to hear was the music of their day, which included everything from Broadway musicals and classical symphonies (I could handle Tchaikovsky, but Chuck Berry's "Roll Over Beethoven" was way cooler) to anything crooned by either Bing Crosby or Ray Noble, to anything penned by either Gershwin or Cole Porter.

Masterful chords and lyrics, to be sure, but just not my style at the time, not when Elvis was belting out "Heartbreak Hotel" right behind the groundbreaking "Rock Around the Clock" by Bill Haley and the Comets.

Then occurred what I think was one of the worst (and best) mistakes my parents made, which they admitted to later on: they bought me a tiny self-contained box-shaped RCA 45 RPM record exchanger—you know, the one with the little sound and the big spindle including a tone-arm that needed a nickel to weigh it down? That machine allowed me the independence to play the rhythm and blues I needed to hear.

I swear to heaven that my mom almost suffered a nervous breakdown when she passed by my room one day and heard Little Richard screaming from the speaker. I can see why; that's a long way from the likes of any tune Johnny Mathis ever recorded, about the only pop my mom could relate to.

"Who and what is that?" she yelled, trying to match Richard's volume but desperately falling short. "Your father and I didn't raise you to be a juvenile delinquent!"

She relaxed somewhat when I played her Fats Domino's "Blueberry Hill," an old standard that at least she could identify with. To add to my mother's misery, I told her I wanted to be a musician, which to her meant a pianist and to me meant the drums, which I eventually took up, leading me to Hollywood for a few years.

As a drummer, and a rock 'n' roller, I felt with great sorrow the passing of two rock 'n' roll legends: Dick Clark and Levon Helm.

Clark, as anyone who ever twisted or ponied or jerked his or her way through their teenage years knows, was the impresario of American Bandstand, a nationally-televised pop music venue designed to show the parents of the younger generation that not all rock 'n' roll was evil, which is kind of amusing when you realize who the first guest he had on his show was.

Performing to clean-cut young prancing boys sporting coats and ties and pretty dancing girls wearing only dresses (never slacks) was "The Killer," wild man Jerry Lee Lewis, who was about as opposite as you could get from the teen idols who came along after Elvis went into the army, Little Richard turned minister, Chuck Berry got arrested for kidnapping, and Buddy Holly died in a plane crash. Lewis himself was banished for marrying his 13 year-old cousin.

The vacuum left by their departures introduced Bobby Rydell, Bobby Darin, Frankie Avalon, Paul Anka, and Fabian, who could never sing worth a darn but he looked the part and sold records. As a matter of fact, just about any act or teen idol that appeared on American Bandstand was almost guaranteed to sell tons of wax.

Clark by this time in the late fifties and early sixties was himself doing quite well, to say the least, having avoided the payola scandal of the time by divesting all his conflicting interests in the record business. The "World's Oldest Teenager" (he was most effective at pitching pimple cream to his audience) had no problem adjusting to the changes in the world of pop music, and to that degree was successful in that the new dance type of rock 'n' roll was far less threatening than its predecessor.

That is until the late sixties, when folk activism and the counter-culture made the scene with acts like Dylan, Jefferson Airplane, Grateful Dead, and Jimi Hendrix.

And lest we forget, the Band, featuring singer-drummer Levon Helm, the master of laidback rhythm and a most sensitive purveyor of lyrics ("The Night They Drove Old Dixie Down") that reduced you to tears, right up until the last waltz.

Thanks for the all the dancing, Dick, and you as well, Levon, for taking the weight off our shoulders.

[April 2012]

Summer Sounds 1

"Roll out those hazy, crazy, lazy days of summer, those days of soda, and pretzels, and beer, you'll wish that summer would always be here."

Summer wouldn't be summer without a summer song. Most of the ones I've heard over the years were meant strictly for Top Forty teenagers, but even the corny, old-fashioned tunes like this one, sung by Nat King Cole, offered themes that almost anyone could relate to, even to young kids like me who preferred sodas to suds.

As a matter of fact, Nat King Cole may have been the only pop artist to have two summer-themed hits in the same season, both in 1963—the other being the elegant "That Sunday, That Summer."

Two other pop singers had notable numbers in a similar innocent style earlier on, during the halcyon days of rock 'n' roll. Steve Lawrence crooned a rather sprightly but stiff "Can't Wait for Summer" in 1957, where he "can't wait for summer to play ball in the park and to park out in the dark."

That was followed two years later by one-hit wonder Jerry Keller, who claimed in "Here Comes Summer" that "School's not so bad but summer's better, gives me more time to see my girl, walks through the park 'neath the shiny moon, when we kiss, she makes my flattop curl." Dated and a bit square, perhaps, but he got his point across.

After all, most summertime recordings revolved around three basic ideas: having fun, picking up girls (or boys), and non-stop partying—unless your fate was like that of rocker Eddie Cochran, who never found a cure for his "Summertime Blues," complaining "Every time I call my baby, and try to get a date, my boss says, no dice son, you gotta work late."

The Beach Boys, Jan and Dean, and Bruce and Terry were the most vocal proponents of this carefree summertime tradition, exemplified by West Coast refrains in the early '60s such as "We've been having fun all summer long," or "Two girls for every boy," in "Surf City," or going to "drive-in movies every night, staying out 'til half past one, sleeping late and living right, cause summer means fun."

On the East Coast, John Sebastian and his Lovin' Spoonful, in their gutsy and gritty 1966 jack-hammer recording of "Summer in the City," beat the humid city heat by venturing out at night as cool cats lookin' for a kitty because "At night it's a different world, go out and find a girl, come-on come-on and dance all night, despite the heat, it'll be alright."

Mungo Jerry announced the arrival of summertime 1970s-style with a lilt slightly more casual and candid: "In the summertime when the weather's high, you can stretch right up and touch the sky, when the weather's fine, you got women, you got women on your mind. Have a drink, have a drive, go out and see what you can find."

The rock group War was even more laid back: "Ridin' 'round town with all the windows down, eight track playin' all your fav'rite sounds, the rhythm of the bongos fill the park, the street musicians tryin' to get a start, 'cause it's summer, my time of year."

There were a few memorable melodies that weren't so sunny. In 1962 Brian Hyland spent a cold and lonely summer writing daily letters "Sealed with a Kiss" to his departed girlfriend. And songstress Carole King didn't fare much better with her beau far away, complaining, "As far as I'm concerned each day's a rainy day so it might as well rain until September."

Chad and Jeremy's "Summer Song" is just downright fatalistic: "They say that all good things must end someday, Autumn leaves must fall, wish you didn't have to go, no, no, no, no."

Overall, however, the summertime song blaring from the transistor or car radio was as fun as the summer itself. My favorite remains the 1958 classic "Summertime, Summertime" ("sum sum summertime") sung by a family quintet calling themselves The Jamies, accompanied only by a harpsichord and a drum: "It's time to head straight for them hills, it's time to live and have some thrills, come along and have a ball, a regular free-for-all. It's summertime."

By the way, all these summer songs are available online. Listen in, but a word of caution: they'll make you wanna dance through the sprinklers.

[August 2009]

Summer Sounds 2

Four years ago about this time, I wrote an article on summertime music—those songs specifically made for seasonal summertime listening, usually tunes with the word "Summer" in the title. "Summer Means Fun," "Summertime, Summertime," "Summertime Blues," "All Summer Long," "A Summer Song," and countless others throughout the years.

But as hit-bound as most of them were, they weren't the songs that defined the summer months from June through August, and perhaps a smidge of September.

From the end of World War II up until 1955, adult "Moon in June" pop songs dominated the charts by combining best sellers in stores, most played by disc jockeys, and most played on juke boxes. Billboard's Hot 100 list wasn't created until late 1955. That year, when Disneyland opened and Davy Crockett and coonskin caps were all the rage, saw a different element appear on the charts, knocking off the giant instrumental and adult-oriented top-seller "Cherry Pink and Apple Blossom White" by Pérez Prado, whose popularity no doubt had been boosted by Cuban bandleader Ricky Ricardo in the TV show *I Love Lucy*.

The new ingredient was rock 'n' roll, and almost all summer long "Rock Around the Clock" by Bill Haley and his Comets owned the top of the charts. Of course, its presence as theme song to the juvenile delinquent movie *The Blackboard Jungle* didn't hurt the cause. Haley's "Clock" kept "Learnin' the Blues," the standard by Frank Sinatra, out of the top spot. Sinatra would reply by saying rock 'n' roll was the work of "cretinous goons."

The summer of 1956 belonged to Elvis, who opened the floodgates with "Heartbreak Hotel" at number one from May 5 through June 16 at seven weeks, and closed the summer in September with "Don't Be Cruel." Sandwiched in between was adult pop fare like Gogi Grant's "The Wayward Wind," the instrumentals "The Poor People of Paris" and "Moonglow," and "I Almost Lost My Mind," another Pat Boone number one, plus "My Prayer" by the popular Platters.

It all belonged to Presley from then on, whose "All Shook Up" and "Teddy Bear" ruled the summertime of 1957, except a strong showing at the top by another Boone hit "Love Letters in the Sand."

Summertime 1958 seemed to be the year of the novelty song, thanks to David Seville (real name Ross Bagdasarian) who created "Witch Doctor" early on that year. Speeding up the tape while singing a vocal, the sound was not unlike a chipmunk ("ooo eee, ooo ah ah, ting tang, walla walla bing bang") which was capitalized on in December with the perennial yuletide favorite "The Chipmunk Song." It was Seville who influenced Sheb Wooley into tracking "The Purple People Eater," which topped the charts for seven weeks from June almost through July. And that was followed by the teenage anthem "Yakety Yak" by the Coasters.

Much of the summer of 1959 was dominated by another novelty song, "The Battle of New Orleans" by honky-tonker Johnny Horton. It was not my favorite; story songs like "The Three Bells," also a smash, get tiring quickly. "Lonely Boy" by Paul Anka was OK, but Fabian's "Tiger" told me that rock 'n' roll had passed.

The summer of 1960 featured the two top female vocalists of the day. Connie Francis with "Everybody's Somebody's Fool" and "My Heart Has a Mind of Its Own," and Brenda Lee with "I'm Sorry" were summertime favorites, as was "Cathy's Clown" by the Everly Brothers. Elvis came out of the Army to sing his next number one, "It's Now or Never," but it was Chubby Checker (Earnest Evans, a chicken-plucker out of Philadelphia who was renamed by Dick Clark's wife as an homage to Fats Domino) who treated the late summer with "The Twist," a dance originally recorded by Hank Ballard.

"The Twist" would also make the top spot in September of the next year, making it the only record to accomplish that feat. Another novelty tune closed the summer of that year: "Please Mr. Custer" by Larry Verne, a stock boy with a voice that just happened to click for producers who today could never get this kind of material on the air.

The summertime of 1961 was owned by an unknown singer named Bobby Lewis, who released the danceable "Tossin' and Turnin'" that was number one in July and August. It followed "Quarter to Three," a Gary U.S. Bonds party record that sounded like it was recorded in a cave.

The year 1962 in my mind was a bust, except for "The Locomotion" by Little Eva, songwriter Carole King's babysitter, and "Sheila" by Buddy Holly sound-alike Tommy Roe.

The beginning and end of the summer of 1963 featured girl group stars Leslie Gore ("It's My Party") and The Angels ("My Boyfriend's Back"), with Jan and Dean's "Surf City" reminding us there were two girls for every boy, and the first live hit to become numero uno: "Fingertips" by Little Stevie Wonder, who headlined at San Francisco's Cow Palace that September but had to leave early because he was underage. The concert booklet that contained his bio said "Stevie was born blind from birth and had a father he rarely saw."

[July 2013]

Summer Sounds 3

Summertime was always, for me anyway, one of the best times to listen to Top Forty radio. There was no school or work if you could avoid it, and if you did catch the summertime blues ("I'm gonna raise a fuss, I'm gonna raise a holler, about workin' all summer just to try to make a dollar") you still had the evenings to cruise in a set of wheels with the radio blaring even if you had no particular place to go—thank you, Chuck Berry.

While there was a host of specific summertime music in the '60s to be heard, a lot of the major hits during June, July, and August had little to do with summer, like "A Hard Day's Night" by the Beatles, "Satisfaction" by the Stones, "Like a Rolling Stone" by Bob Dylan, and countless others, including "Eve of Destruction" by Barry McGuire, "I'm Henry the Eighth I Am" by Herman's Hermits, and "In The Year 2525" by Zager and Evans.

Only one song with the word summer in the title topped the charts in that decade if my memory serves me, and that was probably the best and grittiest summertime record ever made. The production was so exquisite that every time you heard it, you started to sweat. The song, brilliantly written and performed by John Sebastian and the Lovin' Spoonful, was "Summer in the City," complete with sounds of jackhammers and congested car horns in the background.

"Hot town, summer in the city, back of my neck getting dirty and gritty, been down, isn't it a pity doesn't seem to be a shadow in the city, all around, people looking half dead walking on the sidewalk, hotter than a match head . . ." Never been to New York City in the summer? Play this record and it'll put you right there.

Not far behind that 1966 gem was the powerful Motown musical dictum in 1964 that encouraged everyone—including Civil Rights protesters, rioting city dwellers, and the forthcoming counter-culture demonstrating against the Vietnam War—that "Dancing in the Street" was a preferable alternative to the violence occurring along the avenues and the boulevards. "Callin' out around the world, are you ready for a brand new beat? Summer's here and the time is right for dancin' in the street . . ." Let me know if you ever find a resonant sound with a stronger backbeat.

Motown was extremely successful in the summertimes of the '60s: "Heatwave" by the Vandellas, "Mickey's Monkey" by the Miracles, and "Fingertips" by Little Stevie Wonder in '63; "Baby I Need Your Loving" by the Four Tops and "Where Did Our Love Go" by the Supremes in '64; "I Can't Help Myself" and "Back in My Arms" by the same groups in '65; and the same groups again in '66 with "Reach Out" and "You Can't Hurry Love."

The Brits contributed "House of the Rising Sun," and "A Hard Day's Night" in '64; "Help," "Satisfaction," and anything by Peter Noone in '65; and "Sunshine Superman," which I disliked immensely, in '66.

The Beach Boys offered two enormous favorites with "I Get Around" and "California Girls." The folk-rock movement gave us the Byrds, Bob Dylan, the Turtles, and Barry McGuire's controversial "Eve of Destruction," which was banned from the '65 airwaves in a lot of cities.

The Godfather, James Brown, changed the Black music scene dramatically with "Papa's Got a Brand New Bag." So did Percy Sledge with "When a Man Loves a Woman" in '66 and Aretha Franklin in '67 singing and wailing with "Respect." Sock it to me.

That same year saw the emergence of psychedelic sounds offered by the Doors with "Light My Fire" (which I have yet to believe anyone has ever heard straight, if you catch my drift); "Groovin'" by the Rascals (which their record company hated); and the very popular pop tune "Windy" by the Association. One aberration in 1967 was Bobby Gentry's

"Ode To Billie Joe," which radio stations turned into a contest: just what was it that Billie Joe and his girlfriend threw off the Tallahatchie Bridge? It was a well-produced song I must admit, but they played it to death.

Did I mention that the Rat Pack gave us a few summertime scores? Dean Martin hit number one in '64 with "Everybody Loves Somebody Sometime," and Sinatra himself in '66 accomplished a similar feat with "Strangers in the Night." So goes the weird ways of Top Forty radio back then.

If you don't believe me, the decade ended with a summertime bubblegum song, "Sugar Sugar," sending us into the '70s with Mungo Jerry's "In the Summertime."

Summer hasn't been the same since.

[August 2013]

Eve of Destruction

Fifty years ago, the *crème-de-la-crème* of all Top Forty protest sons was recorded and released, much to the consternation of radio programmers from coast to coast, many of whom refused to play it on their airwaves.

I was at the time working for such a man. Ernie Minor owned KKIS, a small Top Forty radio station in Pittsburg, California.

Ernie, who knew I was a teenage rock 'n' roller, sought out my opinion, and I told him I thought he should keep it on the play list, despite pressure from advertisers.

The song in question was "Eve of Destruction," recorded by a former New Christy Minstrels member, gravelly-voiced Barry McGuire.

What's interesting to note are the lyrics, which are just as relevant today as they were then.

Accompanying McGuire were military-like drums, bass and guitar, and harmonica, a perfect blend for a folk message tune of the time:

> *The eastern world it is exploding, violence flarin', bullets loadin'*
> *You're old enough to kill but not for votin'. . .*

Sad to see that not much has changed since 1965.

There was of course an answer record to this diatribe that came out a month later, a wimpy anti-counterculture response, written by the group that produced "At the Hop" by Danny and the Juniors.

It was "Dawn of Correction" by the Spokesmen:

And maybe you can't vote, boy, but man your battle stations
or there'll be no need for votin' in future generations.

You get the idea.

Satirist Tom Leher offers the best idea, calling on his listeners to imagine him accompanying his song on an 88-string guitar since the piano doesn't "qualify" as a folk instrument:

So join in the folk song army, Guitars are the weapons we bring
To the fight against poverty, war, and injustice. Ready! Aim! Sing!

[July 2015]

Kings Go Forth

As a confirmed rock 'n' roller, I was deeply saddened by the recent passings of two glorious American musical giants: both kings, as it were, in their own fields of harmonious expertise.

Singer-songwriter Ben E. King died at the end of April 2015 at 76, and heralded blues guitarist and singer-songwriter B.B. King died May 14, 2015 at 89.

The latter, Mississippi-born and Memphis-raised Riley Ben King (B.B. shortened from "Beale Street Blues Boy" to "Blues Boy") didn't grace the pop charts like Ben E. King at first, but he and his guitar "Lucille" took the blues and rhythm and blues world by storm in the fifties, starting out in dusty juke joints, then later on playing to concert halls up north.

Benjamin Earl Nelson (King), born in North Carolina, then raised in Harlem, came from the vocal group genre. In the late fifties, he and his group were chosen to be the new Drifters, a rhythm and blues vocal ensemble with chart history.

Their first record, "There Goes My Baby," produced by Jerry Leiber and Mike Stoller (the same guys who wrote the original "Hound Dog" and fashioned the Coasters) was thought so awful by label executives that it was shelved for months. But the power of the words and melody (partially written by King), the tympani with its Brazilian Baion rhythm, and the soaring strings (violins on a rock 'n' roll record?) couldn't be denied, and in 1959 it went to number two.

After several dazzling recordings with the Drifters, Ben E. King left a year later to go out on his own and soon scored two major hits.

The first was haunting: "There is a rose in Spanish Harlem, a red rose up in Spanish Harlem. It is the special one, it's never seen the sun. It only comes out when the moon is on the run and all the stars are gleaming . . ."

The second, a few months later, became his signature song: "When the night has come and the land is dark and the moon is the only light we'll see. No, I won't be afraid, oh, I won't be afraid. Just as long as you stand, stand by me." Same Baion beat, similar soaring strings, later introduced to a new generation in Rob Reiner's film of the same name.

As Ben E. King and others of his ilk started to wane because of the English Invasion, the popularity of the blues began rising and it found a whole new audience.

Leading the way of course was B.B. King, who finally hit the upper echelons of the pop charts in late 1969 with this blues classic: "The thrill is gone, the thrill is gone away, the thrill is gone baby. The thrill is gone away, you know you done me wrong baby and you'll be sorry someday."

Want to hear the musical output of two royal musical phenomena? Try YouTube. The thrill is there.

[May 2015]

Sounds of the Season

A call comes in to the KVEC newsroom. Another hot news tip, I hoped, as I picked up the phone.

"Hey, buddy," said the caller, "Enough with the Christmas music already!"

I assumed this guy had heard us earlier broadcast "Little Saint Nick" by the Beach Boys as a lead-in to one of our news segments, this being December first and all.

"You don't like sounds of the Yuletide?" I harked.

"Not when it's played on radio stations 24 hours a day from Thanksgiving on," replied the Scrooge. "It's bad enough it's in all the malls, on ringtones, in commercials. I mean, do I really need to hear 500 renditions of 'White Christmas' by every past and present recording artist who's ever stepped up to a microphone?"

"Why not?" I countered. "You might be exposed to the complete version of the song . . ."

But before I could explain, he hung up. Had he stayed on the line, he would have learned and I would have been glad to tell him that Irving Berlin's classic, which he wrote poolside in July of 1940, is rarely heard in its original form.

Practically all of us are familiar with the "I'm dreaming of a white Christmas, just like the ones I used to know" lyrics best crooned by Der Bingle. But Berlin's prologue has, except for few occasions, always been omitted: "The sun is shining, the grass is green, the orange and palm trees sway. There's never been such a day in Beverly Hills, L-A. But it's December the twenty-fourth, and I am longing to be up north . . ."

To the ardent fan of pop and rock 'n' roll Christmas tunes like me, who has always looked forward to the December musical assault via the airwaves, revelations like these are as exciting as any gift found under the Christmas tree.

Another merry melody, recently revived courtesy of two *Die Hard* movies amusingly enough—and also penned in the summertime by Sammy Kahn in 1945—actually wasn't written for the holidays. "Let It Snow! Let It Snow! Let It Snow!" performed by Vaughn Monroe later that year doesn't mention Christmas in the lyric, but its fireplace charm was eventually adopted as a seasonal song.

My perennial favorite is Nat King Cole's signature 1946 classic "The Christmas Song," written by Mel Torme and Bob Wells—again during another hot summer, this time in 1944—if for nothing else because of its descriptive wintry account: "Chestnuts roasting on an open fire, Jack Frost nipping on your nose, Yuletide carols being sung by a choir, and folks dressed up like Eskimos" to "And so I'm offering this simple phrase, to kids from one to 92, although it's been said many times, many ways, Merry Christmas to you."

If phrases like these can't encourage you to bundle up and spread good cheer, you may not find the North Pole on your GPS this year.

As much as I adore these traditional standards and many others like them (and I mustn't forget "Rudolph the Red-Nosed Reindeer" by Gene Autry), I've always preferred a Christmas that rocked and rolled, going as far back as 1954 when the Drifters, a vocal group from New York, turned "White Christmas" into a rhythm and blues hit that's been around every year since.

And I have to include another doo-wop effort that not too many know about (but I hope they will) called "Christmas in Jail" by the Youngsters in 1956. MADD and the CHP would certainly herald this comical tune about driving under the influence.

The year 1957 seems to be when the rockers started hanging up their stockings, and leave it to Elvis for making that happen with his forlorn recording of "Blue Christmas" along with the raucous "Santa Claus Is Back in Town."

Two country-type hits joined Presley's holiday parade, "Jingle Bell Rock" by Bobby Helms and Brenda Lee's "Rockin' Around the Christmas Tree," both ghosts of Christmas past, present, and, no doubt, future, as is Chuck Berry's fabled guitar-driven "Run, Rudolph, Run."

Christmastime was no stranger to novelty numbers, either, the most successful of those of course being "The Chipmunk Song" with Alvin, Simon, and Theodore.

By the time the sixties came along, almost every rock and roller and teen idol ushered forth a Yuletide vocal or instrumental. In 1963, the Beatles issued their first fan club Christmas good wishes, paving the way for Lennon's political "Happy Christmas (the War is Over)" and McCartney's "Wonderful Christmastime."

The Beach Boys introduced us to Santa's souped-up bobsled, which re-appeared on their Christmas album the following year, and the Four Seasons in characteristic form noted "Santa Clause Is Coming to Town," but it was famed Wall of Sound producer Phil Spector who pulled out all the stops with the release of "A Christmas Gift for You," featuring his stable of girl groups all caroling in their inimitable style, including Darlene Love's incomparable "Christmas (Baby Please Come Home)."

Christmas wouldn't be Christmas if these jewels and countless others old or new weren't shared every year about this time by radio programmers, who I'm delighted to say fill my cup to the brim.

No matter what seasonal sounds you prefer, I wish your stein is as full as mine.

[December 2010]

7

People

Just as infectious was Julia Child, who despite her towering celebrity was just about the most down to earth and highly spirited individual one could ever hope to meet. . . "Never be afraid to make a mistake," I remember her advising me. "And don't worry if whatever you make doesn't turn out."

- Two Tall Ones

Interviewing the Dalai Lama; with Jonathan Winters.

Kuno

It never ceases to amazes me how the multitudes suddenly jump on a bandwagon that's been traveling down the road for years.

Case in point: Tibet, a spiritual land unlike no other which has been under the iron fist of China since 1959, when the Communist country drove out the Dalai Lama and began to systematically plunder and pillage the people and destroy landmarks of his domain.

And it continues to this day. Perhaps it's timing—the Olympic Games awarded to Beijing—or maybe it's technology—hand-held video proof—which hasn't been available until recently. But the struggle isn't anything new. I learned that first-hand from Kuno, a strange and wise Tibetan fellow whom I first met in Santa Barbara in 1990.

Kuno was the Dalai Lama's primary biographer when I was first introduced to him. When he wasn't traveling with the Dalai Lama promoting peace and freedom for their country, he would wander the world on his own, carrying his non-violent message wherever he could. In one of his satchels were hundreds of brightly-colored Tibetan flags, which he would hand out to supporters of his cause.

There was a time in Kuno's life, however, when all was not peaceful, he once admitted to me.

When China interceded in Tibetan affairs in 1951, Kuno, who spoke fluent Chinese and was adept in political affairs, was appointed Tibetan ambassador to the Maoist country. During the next eight years, he gained diplomatic respectability and made hundreds of notable friends.

When relations between the two countries deteriorated, the Chinese invaded Tibet, forcing the Dalai Lama and other spiritual leaders to hurriedly flee to Dharamsala in India. Kuno was among the throng, but his family couldn't get out in time. Kuno was eventually to learn that his mother, father, and other family members were tortured and slaughtered by the Chinese in the aftermath, a ferocious act of such betrayal that Kuno told me he would never forgive Chinese people anywhere.

Having turned against all the Chinese friends he had made, Kuno kept this resentment for many years, until he interviewed with the Dalai Lama, who was looking for a biographer.

Kuno was appointed to the position, but not before being told that his hatred had been misplaced. "Besides," humored the Dalai Lama as only he could, "Look at all the great Chinese food you've been missing over the years."

My attempts at contacting Kuno the last few years have fallen short, I'm sad to say, but there was a time when we did spend a lot of time together. If we weren't sharing dinner at our house, it would always be at a Chinese restaurant. It was a good idea to get to know the Chinese again, he confided, always with a grin. I had no doubt where he got that from.

Having been graced with Kuno's presence, it was only a matter of time before I would one morning be graced with the presence of the subject of his biography. What struck me most about the Dalai Lama during our small audience was not just his endless compassion, perspective, and conviction, but his humor.

"What is it like knowing that the only thing you can be is the Dalai Lama?" I asked him.

After less than a moment, he looked at me and answered, with a twinkle in his eye, "I have no choice." Then he laughed.

How Kuno was going to put that kind of commitment into words was a mystery to me, I told him, as we engaged on one of the many long hikes we would take in the mountainous terrain of the back country above Santa Barbara. Along the many trails, I tried to absorb every pearl of wisdom he had to offer.

"You must take care of yourself," he advised me more than once. "Your body is a sacred temple."

His curiosity was so abundant, we often stopped and wondered more than we wandered. "What kind of flower is this?" he would always want to know. "We don't have plants anything like this in India. But we do have mountains. You must come to my country to hike. I invite you."

I didn't tell Kuno that my idea of a hike did not include Sherpas or oxygen tanks.

But it was his serenity, I recall, that was most deafening, especially during those moments we exchanged in silence as we would sit on a rocky ledge overlooking the canyons that crept all the way to the sea.

Here we would meditate, after having climbed down from the top of the Santa Ynez Mountain range, where Kuno had taken a green Tibetan flag from his pouch and posted it on a tree atop La Cumbre Peak, 4,000 feet above humanity. And for humanity.

[April 2008]

The Big W

To me, he was always Maude Frickert, or Elwood P. Suggins, or Lennie Pike (the furniture mover in *Mad Mad World* searching for the Big W), but I rarely knew him as Jonathan Winters, who passed away last week. Few people did, even all his friends and patrons at the Montecito Barber Shop, a joint he often frequented.

I first met Jonathan or one of his many zany characters early on in my life via the record player. Winters, along with other prominent comedians of the day like Bob Newhart and Shelley Berman, got the attention of the public by either appearing at hip nightclubs or waxing their craft on long-playing records. Jonathan's titles pretty much said it all about the kind of funny and creative man he really was: *Another Day Another World*, *Humor Seen Through the Eyes of*, *Here's Jonathan* (with Winters in different garbs) and strangely enough, *Down To Earth*.

It was during this time, legend has it, that Winters (portraying Maude Frickert, an old lady character he developed from his days in the Midwest), climbed the tower of the Ferry Building in San Francisco and stayed there until he was eventually talked down and carried off to a funny farm for several months. Whether or not this particular event is true (Winters has himself acknowledged spending several months in a psychiatric institution twice early in his career), it fits right in, to me anyway, with his crazy personae.

Winter's strength was his uncanny ability to improvise on the spot; he could be anything or anybody at any time. He was also a master of mimicry, playing his favorite actors from the past, usually odd ones like Boris Karloff or Eugene Paulette.

Winters himself was considered an off-beat character, endlessly preferring the hipsters to the squares. The only humorous antics you missed on his Verve recordings, and there were quite a few, were his bizarre facial contortions which were comedy lines unto themselves. But Winters made up for it with all the eccentric sound effects he could muster. On one album, *The Wonderful World of Jonathan Winters*, all his sounds were listed, as though they were as vital as the skits he performed.

The skits, by the way, were created from all the movies he'd seen growing up as a boy in Ohio, whether they be westerns or musicals, or from personal experiences, such as his two-and-a-half year stint in the Marine Corps during World War II. All were the tallest of tales. And all made you howl.

Jonathan Winters and I began our acquaintance in the early 1990s while I was still a news anchor for KEYT-TV in Santa Barbara. One of my assignments at the time was producing a local offshoot of an ABC special on comedy called *What Makes People Laugh*. Who better to interview than Jonathan Winters?

So I went over to his spread in nearby Montecito, where I was graciously shown around and introduced to his varied interests that few people (including myself) knew he engaged in, like his historic gun collection and his artwork.

Then we sat down outside on his back patio and proceeded with our discussion.

About this time a small airplane (like a Cessna) began to fly right over where we were sitting, making it impossible to hear our dialogue. Each time it did, Winters would remark something like "Boy if I had one of my Civil War cannons he wouldn't be up there very long" or "Come down here and fight like a man, you son of a gun." Winters actually said something a bit stronger, but as a rule he never swore during any routine.

We never got around to answering the question "What makes people laugh?"

We didn't have to. Jonathan's improv on the airplane pilot spoke volumes.

That Winters was a major influence on standup comedy doesn't really need to be mentioned. All you really need to experience is Robin Williams, who is Winters at 78 RPM.

But experiencing Jonathan Winters changes your life.

What's your definition of down to earth? Here is his, from his first album cover:

> I have no real verbal gems to pass along,
> only to say this: I live for now—24 hours
> at a time. I've tried being a lot of things,
> assuming all kinds of roles, but I've come
> to the conclusion that in the long run
> "being down to Earth" is the answer for me.
> Oh, it leaves you wide open to criticism
> but as far as I'm concerned it makes living
> with yourself a hell of a lot easier!

Thanks for the advice, Big W.

[April 2013]

Kind to the Very End

Boy did I miss a lot of big news while I was away in Vietnam.

Forty years ago this summer, I left the good old USA for a year-long commitment in Saigon. I wouldn't return to The World, a G.I. reference to the states, for 365 days, provided of course that I lived through the entire experience.

To allay that fear, one of the first things I did after arriving was to seek counsel from a soldier who was headed home. I asked him, "What are my chances of staying alive in Saigon for a year as a blonde-haired, blue-eyed American English language instructor decked out in U.S. military jungle fatigues with an M-16 strapped to my back?"

He replied, quite casually, and with a grin to boot, "Your odds of surviving here are probably better here than in New York City." Ludicrous or amusing, it was an answer I could handle.

Good thing he prepped me, too, because two weeks later, one of our two schools was blown to bits. It was going to be a hell of a long tour.

While stories of that ilk along with other in-country events like Ho Chi Min's death and the My Lai Massacre would continue to make head-lines stateside for the next year, the news from the home front during that period wasn't any less absurd, zany, or unbelievable: Armstrong's lunar leap, Kennedy's Chappaquiddick, Woodstock's tunes, Altamont's dirge, Kent State's bullets, Isla Vista's bank blaze, and the Beatles' swan song.

But the story that hit home the most involved a childhood neighbor I grew up with.

I read about it in the San Francisco Chronicle, sent to me four days late but providing me with a familiar sense of what was going on in my hometown and the rest of the country.

Taking a break from class one morning, I picked up the August 10 edition and saw a headline: "Actress among five slain at home in Beverly Hills." On the second page were photos of the victims. One I immediately recognized. I jumped out of my chair.

"My Lord," I stammered, "That's Gibby Folger! What was she doing there?"

Reading further in amazement, details revealed that coffee heiress Abigail Folger, along with her boyfriend Wojciech Frykowski, was indeed present at the Cielo Drive residence of actress Sharon Tate where five savage and brutal murders took place. Gibby was reportedly stabbed to death, two days shy of her 26th birthday.

I was stunned. I looked away. It wasn't that long ago when our paths crossed. The last time I had seen her was two years earlier in San Francisco, where she lived briefly not far from my mom.

At the time, she was working at the UC Art Museum in Berkeley. I'd known Gibby for years. Our families were old friends, living not far apart from each other in Woodside, California, where we grew up.

The Folgers may have been wealthy, but you'd never guess it knowing Gibby. She was as down to earth as they come, as was her younger brother Peter, one of my more competitive playmates at that time.

I always remember Gibby as being quite gracious, affable, and attractive. She was also intelligent, gifted, and very athletic, especially in tennis and horseback riding. Not a summer went by it seemed without our waving to each other as she would trot by on one of the many equestrian trails in our neighborhood.

With my cousin Caroline, who often rode with her, she attended Santa Catalina School in Monterey, later graduated from Radcliffe, and eventually earned an art history degree from Harvard, leading to the job she had when we bumped into one another. She hinted to me that she was thinking about soon moving to New York, just to get away for a while.

That was the last time we talked.

I resumed reading. The rest of the sensational account in the Chronicle couldn't offer much more information, the crime having just occurred. It was reported that Tate, like Gibby, was stabbed, along with Frykowski and hairstylist Jay Sebring, who were shot as well. Steven Parent, visiting caretaker William Garretson, also was gunned down. Garretson was taken into custody as a suspect. The word "PIG" was scribbled in blood on the front door of the Benedict Canyon house.

What the hell had happened, and why, I wondered.

The next night, the La Biancas would be murdered in similar fashion. Several months later Charles Manson and his family were linked to the crimes.

By that time, I learned that Gibby had followed up on her move to New York, where she met Frykowski. A year later, they moved to Los Angeles, where Gibby, the ever-compassionate socialite, got heavily involved in volunteer social work in the ghettos.

It was Wojciech who introduced Gibby to Roman Polanski and his wife Sharon Tate, who invited the pair to move in. After several months, Gibby and Wojciech were all set to leave when Sharon asked them if they could both stay one more weekend until Roman got home from Europe.

Never one to turn down a friend, Gibby agreed.

Little could she know it would be her last act of kindness.

[August 2009]

Two Tall Ones

One of the most engaging aspects of being a journalist is getting the opportunity to know some of the fascinating people you meet.

Anchoring television news in a beautiful market like Santa Barbara doesn't hurt either. This particular Mediterranean-style paradise has always attracted more than its share of celebrities, many of whom visit, then decide to settle down.

Two that come to mind because of recent news events are Fess Parker, who sadly passed away last week, and Julia Child, recently lionized in the film *Julie & Julia*.

I first met Fess long before he built the Red Lion (now Doubletree) Inn along Santa Barbara's waterfront. I was doing a story on a mobile home park he owned. Fess, needless to say, was larger than life, literally and figuratively. I never imagined that Davy Crockett was an imposing six-foot-six.

About his portrayal as the fabled Tennessean in Walt Disney's groundbreaking *King of the Wild Frontier* television series in the fifties, Parker would later tell me that despite the worldwide fame and acclaim he received from the role, he hardly saw a dime.

"Mr. Disney was a genius, and I've always appreciated the opportunity he gave me," said Fess in his familiar Texas drawl, describing how he was chosen for the part after Disney spotted him in the 1954 science fiction cinematic thriller *THEM!*.

"But I never made any money playing Davy Crockett. I made sure that never happened again. When *Daniel Boone* came along, I owned 30 percent of the series."

After that television show ran its course in 1970, Fess left Hollywood and moved to Santa Barbara in the mid-seventies to pursue business interests involving several controversial real estate activities, along with a winery and restaurant in the Santa Ynez Valley. He may have disappeared from the silver screen, but he would never be out of the spotlight from then on.

"I guess I rub some people the wrong way," an understatement he once admitted to me, referring to his longstanding battles with the city and environmentalists over several contentious developments he pursued.

When I gave him a VHS copy of *THEM!*, in which he plays a pilot claiming to have seen giant nuclear mutated queen ants flying alongside his airplane (subsequently forcing authorities to detain him in a padded cell) he humorously remarked, "Thanks, King. I can't think of anything more appropriate. This is where some folks think I ought to be, locked up in a loony bin."

Fess was anything but batty—he was crazy like a fox, with a stubborn streak as prominent as that stripe you might find on one of his coonskin caps.

Nonetheless, it was hard not to like Fess. He was one of the most gracious and endearing gentlemen I've ever had the pleasure to be acquainted with.

Just as infectious was Julia Child, who despite her towering celebrity was just about the most down to earth and highly spirited individual one could ever hope to meet. Of course, Julia was no stranger to me (or hardly anyone else in the world) by the time that I met her; she had become a household icon cooking up French cuisine on PBS.

So I naturally was very surprised to see her wandering the aisles of Vons in Montecito in 1981.

"What are you doing here?" I asked, quite taken aback at seeing her in my neck of the woods.

"My husband Paul and I just bought a condominium in Bonny Doon, next to the Biltmore," she replied in that unmistakable warbly voice. "Winters can get so cold in Boston."

She graciously agreed to her first local TV interview with me, where she and Paul discussed their storied life together and Julia's rise to prominence as the French Chef. "Never be afraid to make a mistake," I remember her advising me, "and don't worry if whatever you make doesn't turn out."

A few weeks later, Julia repeated those words when my wife Sara and I came over for dinner.

That delightful experience, the first of many we shared over the years after the Childs settled in Santa Barbara, was memorable for several reasons, not the least of which was the familial atmosphere that only Julia could provide.

Being with her was like being at home with a humorously gifted great aunt who loved to clatter around with all the pots and pans, unafraid to get her hands into the mix.

We all had a task to do. Paul, who I was amazed to learn was a karate expert on top of his photographic talents, would provide the anecdotes; Sara would help set the table or answer the phone; I would put away Julia's kitchen utensils on a specially made peg board; all the while she was devising everything divine from poached salmon to an après-dinner chocolate soufflé, which, when it failed to rise to the occasion, elicited an unflappable reaction only Julia could cook up: "Dear me! I believe we are having apples and cheese for dessert, everyone."

Years later Julia told me her secret to life was to cook, to eat, and to live. What a recipe to pass on that is. Enjoy with a bottle of Fess Parker Red and *Bon Appétit*!

[March 2010]

Hillman Country

Those of us like me who came of age in the turbulent 1960s were constantly looking for some kind of harmony in a world fraught with all kinds of discord. I found it by simply turning on the radio.

In the spring of 1965, I experienced an unfamiliar sound, a folk song with a rock 'n' roll beat. Some band had taken the Bob Dylan ballad "Hey Mr. Tambourine Man," electrified it with amplified guitars, a protruding bass, and a solid snare, and then layered it with soaring and ethereal vocals.

The ensemble that committed this musical transgression (according to folk purists, certainly), was a group called The Byrds, whose effort shot to the top of the charts and has since been labeled the record that started the folk-rock movement.

Former Byrd base player Chris Hillman, who recently recorded an album produced by Tom Petty and Herb Pedersen, is still playing the music he loves, in the studio and live on stage. The 72-year-old musician once told me it made sense at the time.

"Most of us, Roger (Jim) McGuinn, David Crosby, Gene Clark, and myself had roots in folk music, everyone from the Weavers to the Kingston Trio," he said. "I was also influenced by country hillbilly and bluegrass, playing the mandolin.

"When they asked me to join, they were looking for a bass guitar player. I never touched a bass before but I of course didn't tell them that. At the same time, I assumed they were proficient with electric guitars, but the band was basically acoustic save for Roger's electric Rickenbacker, quite distinguishable on a danceable version of 'Mr.

Tambourine Man' cut with LA studio musicians because we were still working building up our sound."

By the time the band recorded what Hillman calls their signature tune—"Turn! Turn! Turn!"—a few months later, The Bryds were flying high, having created a uniquely eclectic sound featuring two major elements that defined their sound: Roger McGuinn's jangling and melodic Rickenbacker 12-string electric guitar and the group's complex vocal characteristics heard on hits like "It Won't Be Wrong," "Eight Miles High," and "My Back Pages."

Hillman's contribution to the group as a singer-songwriter wasn't fully realized until the group's fourth album, *Younger than Yesterday*, was released in 1967.

"The cobwebs came off after I played some jazzy musical sessions with South African composer Hugh Masakela, whose rhythm and trumpet playing we used on one of the first songs I wrote with Roger called 'Rock 'n' Roll Star,'" Hillman said about a classic number that fairly accurately described The Byrds themselves at full throttle.

Hillman, who today lives in Ventura, won't disagree that his life with The Byrds at their pinnacle didn't resemble their influential anthem.

"It was true," he claims. "Girls were really chasing us. It was exactly like the Beatles movie *A Hard Day's Night*. We were really living it."

Hillman composed another rocker for the album, "Have You Seen Her Face," followed by two songs that revealed his country roots, setting the stage for the group's next country-oriented album *Sweetheart of the Rodeo*, which opened doors for country rock bands like the Eagles, and that of his own personal musical direction, which included, after leaving The Bryds, involvement in The Flying Burrito Brothers, Manassas, Souther-Hillman-Fura-Band, among others.

It was not until the surprising success of the country band Desert Rose that things finally jelled. "We had a good eight-year run," he said, "And were accepted by Nashville for what we did, not for who we had been."

The passionate Hillman, who was inducted into the Rock & Roll Hall of Fame in 1991 and is one of the most engaging rock 'n' roll personas I've ever met, continues to perform. He says his best work lies ahead, an enthusiastic affirmation you can clearly detect in his voice.

"I've had a great career which is still going strong. Now I mentor and teach, giving back with everything I learned.

"I really believe this is the best time in my life."

[April 2017]

Unlucky Lindy

It was called at the time, and for many years following, the Crime of the Century.

In the stormy evening hours of March 1, 1932, the first-born 20-month-old baby boy of famous aviator Charles "Lucky Lindy" Lindbergh was snatched from his crib in his room on the second floor of the rural Lindberg home in East Amwell, New Jersey, by someone bent on getting $50,000 for the child's safe return.

"Wanted," read circulating flyers and posters, "Information to the whereabouts of Chas. A. Lindbergh, Jr. This child was kidnapped from his home between 8 and 10 p.m. on Tuesday, March 1, 1932. Age 20 months, weight 30 pounds, height 29 inches, hair curly blond, eyes dark blue, complexion light with a deep dimple in the center of chin, dressed in one-piece coverall night suit."

In April, the ransom was paid, netting no results.

On May 12, the body of a child later identified by the aviator as his son was discovered by two passing truck drivers well off a road in some woods about two miles from the Lindbergh home. Lindbergh ordered the body cremated following an autopsy that revealed his son had died from a skull fracture.

In September 1934, after an exhaustive investigation, police arrested a German immigrant carpenter for spending some of the $14,000 traceable ransom money that had been found in his garage next to his home in the Bronx. Bruno Richard Hauptman, despite maintaining his innocence throughout, was charged with the crime, convicted, and eventually electrocuted in April of 1936.

Justice in the case may have been served, except for one small detail: the Lindbergh baby was never kidnapped. That's if you believe Charles Augustus Lindbergh, Jr., very much alive and well today, who claims that he is the baby that was supposedly abducted.

Lindbergh, who contacted me recently because he used to listen to KVEC while spending his high school days in San Luis Obispo during the 1940s, adamantly disputes the pages of history.

"There was never any kidnapping. My father orchestrated my disappearance that night. I was a physically imperfect child, born with hammertoes, and because he was a Nazi who believed in the Aryan race, couldn't stand the sight of me, so he had me secretly spirited out of the house. From that point on, I lived with several different families all over the country for the next 30 years. I was in reality an orphan all that time."

"So you're saying that no intruder ever entered the house, that the crude wooden ladder leading up to the nursery outside the house was a prop, and the kidnapping was staged, ultimately resulting in the death of an innocent man?" I asked.

"Yes, orchestrated by my father, who was very cold-hearted."

"Then who was the kid whose decomposed body was found?"

"Probably from a graveyard. The dirt on the body didn't match the dirt where it was found, and the body was three inches taller than I was, but my father was the only one who identified it, and then had it immediately cremated."

"So what makes you think that you are really Charles Lindberg, Jr.?"

"For one thing, my facial features resemble those of my father, I possess the same physical characteristics of my brothers and sisters, like flat fingernails and freckled, superfluously fleshy hands and knuckles, and I have overlapping toes like the Lindbergh baby.

"For another, reliable sources throughout my life have told me directly that I am indeed the Lindbergh baby.

"For example, Jay Langley, editor of the Hunterdon County Democrat newspaper, who was very familiar with the Lindbergh baby kidnapping and the events following, said to me in 1988, 'Charlie, you are the son the Colonel did not want.'

"While I attended San Luis Obispo High School and then studied aeronautics at the community college there, I also worked at Austin's Restaurant, and my boss told his wife that he was to take me to a coffee shop nearby to be observed by Colonel Lindbergh and an FBI agent. He said to her 'The FBI thinks he might be the kidnapped Lindbergh boy.'

"There have been dozens of others. Over the course of many years, I was frequently the subject of constant observation by the FBI, which won't disclose the complete files of the Lindbergh kidnapping case, fearing it will cause embarrassment to their investigation and that the privacy of certain individuals, like members of my family, might be invaded. And in 1997 I took a lie detector test administered by a licensed polygraph examiner in Santa Maria who concluded with no doubt that I was telling the truth."

"So why don't members of your family who are still living simply provide DNA samples to determine your identity?"

"Because they all know I am Charles Lindbergh, Jr., and they would have to cut me in on the family fortune. It's the money. My siblings don't want to split the money."

He could use some, apparently. Today Lindbergh is flat broke, living with his wife's relatives in Cupertino. An attorney has tried to prove his case, several accounts have been written about Lindbergh's claim, and a documentary about his story is being planned for release soon.

One thing's for sure: Lindbergh's got more fortitude than the Spirit of St. Louis.

[January 2011]

The Fighting Irish

Everyone has dreams and desires.

Mo Clancy's was to participate in the Boston Marathon in 2006. When she wasn't working at her job as a physical education counselor for Arroyo Grande Hospital, she was off jogging somewhere training for the run of a lifetime. She qualified, and was set to go when she ran right into an unexpected hurdle.

"It was Christmas week of 2005. I developed urinary retention and I was chalking it up to the fatigue and malaise of old age," she said. "I didn't think much of it.

"Then on New Year's morning, after a five-mile run, I developed a right-side ache. When I got to work the next day, I started hunching over. So I went to emergency, had some tests done, and that's when I got the news. My doctor told me they found a very large mass in my pelvic region. They suspected ovarian cancer."

While having ovarian cancer is not necessarily an automatic death sentence, it is the deadliest of all gynecologic cancers and the fifth leading cause of cancer deaths among American women. That's because it's one of the hardest to spot.

For every 20,000 women who are diagnosed with the disease every year, 15,000 will die. The tools and methods that exist for early detection of breast and cervical cancers are not yet available for ovarian cancer.

"My doctor said that even if I had taken a Pap smear in the July before Christmas, it might not have shown up. It can grow that quickly; it's that hard to detect.

They ran a test on me called the CA125 and told me it was elevated.

I was beyond stages one and two, which affects mainly just the ovaries. Here your survival rate is much greater. I had stage three, and was told I would require a total hysterectomy. They'd take out the ovaries, the uterus, and would cleanse the whole area as much as they could to get all the cancer cells. My survival rate would not be as certain. After surgery and chemotherapy, you see how long you can go without it coming back. The longer the better."

Mo, who was in her mid-forties at the time, underwent immediate surgery and completed a grueling chemotherapy treatment by June of 2006. The cancer reappeared two years later.

"They found a recurrence in September 2008. The longer there's no recurrence the better the chance it won't come back. I wasn't too surprised, because at stage three it's more likely than not. It was good that it was two years."

Mo told me that she had put her own health on the back burner because she was so busy taking care of her ailing parents, particularly her mom, who eventually died from lung cancer in 2004 following her father's passing in 2003.

"I have to say, watching my own mother go through her own journey with cancer has given me the spirit and determination to continue with my life; she never complained, and always put one foot in front of the other.

"I always keep my mom in mind. I feel the strength I have in walking through this is my mom. I want to be proud enough to be able to walk through this with as much dignity as I can. I do believe a positive attitude helps through your journey."

Mo's journey included a trip to the altar. "I met Seamus two weeks before I was diagnosed. We looked at each other and I said, 'I don't know where this is going. You can come along for the ride. We'll see where it takes us.'

"It took us to Ireland where Seamus was from, as was my father. We were married in 2006 in a church with a reception in a castle."

And despite her disease, Mo, like her mother, kept putting one foot in front of the other, determined to run in the Boston Marathon, a goal delayed by her diagnosis. In April of 2007, she achieved her dream.

"I started jogging again after chemo. Time was no longer the big deal. I just wanted to finish it. When you see that Sitco sign with two miles to go, you know you have it. Seamus was standing at the finish line. When I saw that Sitco sign, I had a tear in my eye. I thought of my folks and thought this is the beginning of a new life. If I can do this, I can beat cancer."

Mo no longer jogs, but continues to take things in stride. She is now busy as ever getting the word out about her disease during September, Ovarian Cancer Awareness Month. Turning up the volume, she says, helps raise funding for detection resources.

"To be perfectly honest, I find that my diagnosis has been a blessing. It has helped me to move on and to realize how important every single day is."

[September 2009]

Surviving a Bullet

I don't know what Heaven or Hell must be like, but I know one man who does, and he is worth remembering on Holocaust Remembrance Day, or Yom Hashoa, which occurs on May 2.

"The Holocaust is not merely a story of destruction and loss; it is a story of an apathetic world and a few rare individuals of extraordinary courage," reads a passage on the United States Holocaust Memorial Museum website. "It is a remarkable story of the human spirit and the life that flourished before the Holocaust, struggled during its darkest hours, and ultimately prevailed as survivors rebuilt their lives."

Thomas Toivi Blatt is one such survivor. When he was 15, he was one of 50 captive Polish Jews who escaped from Sobibor, one of Germany's first death camps (along with Treblinka and Belzec) and lived to talk about his experience and the prisoner revolt that freed him.

When I first met Blatt in 1987, he was living on the Central Coast as the owner of a car stereo shop. I interviewed him a week before a major motion picture film about his plight, *Escape from Sobibor*, was televised. In the film, he was portrayed as a young teenage boy nicknamed Toivi, who managed to avoid the gas chambers at the Polish prison because he was skilled at making and repairing shoes and clothes, a "necessity" for the German SS officers operating the compound.

Blatt told me that a day didn't go by when he didn't see or smell the smoke or the stench from the stacks of the six gas chambers that were filled with carbon monoxide and used ultimately to exterminate 250,000 men, women, and children during the 18-month existence of the camp, from April 1942 until October 14, 1943.

On that day a revolt caused it to be shut down, liquidated, and disguised as a farm, which is one reason Sobibor wasn't as notorious as Auschwitz or Dachau: there was nothing left behind for the Allies to find.

Blatt was not only among the 300 Jewish prisoners to escape during the infamous uprising, but he played a major role in helping to execute the daring plot.

In my interview with Blatt, he said he was instructed to lure some of the SS guards to their death in order for the breakout to succeed. The plan was to eliminate all the SS officers and as much of the Ukrainian Army guards as possible, so that hopefully 600 inmates could escape.

Blatt and his conspirators killed 11 SS soldiers and a number of Ukrainians before the Germans discovered their dead, but not before 300 of the inmates scaled and broke through the fences, running for their lives towards the nearby forest. Few survived to the end of the war, but some, like Blatt, well beyond. Most of his compatriots were either killed in the mine fields surrounding the camp or subsequently hunted down and shot.

Even though Blatt made it to the trees, he was far from out of the woods. He recalled to me that as the Germans were on his tail, he and a fellow escapee made it to what they thought was the safety of a barn at a nearby farmhouse, only to find to their surprise and horror that the owner, although Polish, was partisan to the Nazi cause.

The farmer "secured" a hiding place underground in the barn, and then tried to bury Blatt and his friend alive, but when they dug themselves free, the farmer returned with his rifle and shot both men in the head.

Blatt was left for dead. The bullet that was supposed to kill him remains in his jaw to this day.

"Here, King, you can still feel the bullet," he offered during our dialogue.

As I touched the hidden slug nestled just behind the front of his jaw-bone, I couldn't help but feel as well absolute amazement at how this man could have possibly survived his incredible and terrifying ordeal.

Today, Blatt lives in Seattle, Washington. He has written two books on his experiences at Sobibor, one entitled *Sobibor: The Forgotten Revolt.* He also created a website which bears an inscription from words spoken by Aleksander Aronowich Perchersky, one of the leaders of the Sobibor revolt, with a young Blatt right by his side, seconds before the outbreak:

"Those of you who may survive, bear witness, let the rest of the world know what has happened here."

[May 2008]

8

Santa Barbara

There was a time last century when kids wearing cocked hats with newspapers in hand would cry out and hawk the dailies of the day from street corners and newsstands in major cities across America. No longer, sadly, but if that era were to return, the same kids on the street corners of Santa Barbara trying to sell the Santa Barbara News-Press would most likely be hollering "Extra! Extra! Read all about nothing!"

~Feud and Folly

Expires December 31, 1980

KING HARRIS
Name
KEYT TV
Affiliation
SANTA BARBARA, CA
Location

Kim. King.

KEYT-TV
Channel
3

KEY NEWS
6 & 11 P.M.

The team that delivers Ventura County's news!

Debby

It was May of 1990. At the time, I was news director and anchor at KEYT-TV in Santa Barbara and I was looking for a co-anchor to replace Paula Lopez, who had left for Hollywood. The phone rang.

"Hello, this is King."

"Mr. Harris, this is Deborah Davison calling from Tucson. I understand you have an opening for an anchor?"

"We sure do. Send me a tape and resume and I'll get back to you."

"Will do. Thanks. Bye."

It took me less than a minute before I realized who it was that called me. Holy Smokes! I had just talked with Debby Davison, whom I had seen over the years as an anchor at KTLA Channel 5 in Los Angeles.

Could I acquire a major market TV news personality for small market KEYT? I called her right back and told her to come up and see me, which she did.

Despite a limited budget (to say the least), I knew I had several things going for me: I had a resourceful and tremendous general manager in Sandy Benton; we had an award-winning news department with great photographers and reporters; we were in scenic Santa Barbara; and Debby was frustrated and disillusioned with the profession.

By that I mean it ain't easy being a woman in a male-dominated profession where at too many stations the male anchors present all the hard news and the females read all the fluff. I learned a long time ago, despite the whims of consultants, that women were just as credible and capable, some even more so than their male counterparts.

Working with the highly spirited Christine Craft taught me that.

On set, even. I remember tossing it to our sports guy at the time: "Well, Mike, I guess the big word in sports tonight is *déjà vu*."

At which Christine blurted out, "That's not one word, that's two words!" Nuff said.

Debby Davison was just as emphatic, in her own stylish way. She was precise and meticulous, if not nearly perfect. She was well-spoken and articulate. And in addition to being a skilled reporter, she was also a great interviewer and a very good listener.

She shined particularly bright in all of the telethons we did, especially Christmas Unity where she out-sparkled all the lights, ornaments, and poinsettias—even the tree.

What set Debby apart, I think, was one quality that you rarely see in television news, big market or small: she was a class act.

Which is why I didn't mind at all meeting one of her requests upon her hiring, that she and I would exchange openings to the news every other night: "KEY News with Debby Davison and King Harris" one night, then the next evening "KEY News with King Harris and Debby Davison."

Even our advisors, Frank Magid and Associates, the top TV news consulting firm in the world, didn't seem to mind.

They *were* bothered by one thing out of the blue one day. Frank called me up from his Montecito home and said to me, "King, we at Magid just discovered something very interesting. On the set, you sit on Debby's left, correct? We think you should switch chairs so she is on your right, because we have found that since the viewer's eyes go left to right, it establishes a superior presence for the male."

I shot back, "Frank, if you want to tell Debby Davison that she should change anchor chairs, you go right ahead. I'm not touching that with a ten-foot pole."

The only time I can remember Debby next to me on my right was when we were both out on the patio behind the newsrooms covering the Painted Cave fire, which broke out not long after she got to KEYT. She had yet to find her way around Santa Barbara but in giving out information, especially under the circumstances, you would never know that. She was a real pro that way.

What often amused me about her were some of her quirks. For example, I learned that if we were sitting on the set together and she started furiously tapping her pencil on the desktop, she was peeved about something I'd hear about later. Or watching her reaction one time to our eccentric meteorologist Phil Mann's diatribe about his uncle being struck not once but twice by lightning, leaving him with two big holes in his stomach. It was priceless. Her jaw dropped, her mouth opened, and her eyes nearly sprang out of her head, as if she were saying, "Why is Phil telling me this?"

And Debby, being the Boston Catholic she was, wasn't endeared to certain news stories that were rather risqué, tales like those involving husband-hating knife-wielding Lorena Bobbitt.

I can't say I blame her; I wasn't comfortable reading them either.

Debby preferred local news because she cared so much about the community. She proudly served KEYT for 16 years.

I was greatly saddened to hear about her death recently after a courageous years-long battle with breast cancer. At the same time, I was grateful to have had the opportunity to work alongside her.

She raised everyone's standards, including my own.

Thank God she called.

[July 2015]

Unity

Of all the events I've experienced in my career over the years as a news journalist, none will ever quite compare to that of helping to create—and participating in—a seasonal event televised by KEYT-TV in Santa Barbara that became known as the Christmas Unity Telethon.

Its stage was both inside the studio and outside on the patio of the facility, high up on a mesa referred to as "TV Hill" overlooking the city.

With music provided by talent from local school choirs to popular musicians and singers far and wide (persuaded by those who already lived in the area), it blossomed into an incredible 12-hour community celebration of seasonal spirit and Yuletide cheer, underscored by the cause: to help a multitude of less fortunate who otherwise might not experience any kind of Christmas whatsoever.

It was a bold undertaking. I don't to this day know specifically whose idea it was, but it had its seeds in one charitable woman named Barbara Tellefsen, who for many a year had been collecting toys, clothing, and food for those in need at her tiny Christmas Unity store downtown.

What if, she suggested to my more than receptive station manager Sandy Benton in the fall of 1987, we could get all the various nonprofit agencies like Food Bank, Salvation Army, Toys for Tots, and others to come together under one umbrella called "Christmas Unity" and work as one organization to ensure that gifts would be distributed equally and efficiently?

And what if KEYT could provide some valuable airtime like a telethon to raise funds for the cause?

Good ideas on both counts, ones that would come to fruition when

Montecito resident and super songster Kenny Loggins entered the picture. He suggested, in his quiet, unassuming manner, that he could gather a whole bunch of musicians like himself who would perform for the event, free of charge, thereby ensuring a strong and wide audience. Who could turn down such a generous offer?

So while Loggins set out to contact his playmates, including former partner Jim Messina, and while then-KEYT production manager Don Katich corralled his crew for the monumental task of producing the program, Benton, Tellefsen, and I went out to encourage and convince all the independent and territorial nonprofits to join the Unity collective.

There were of course a few egos that had to be converted.

One was a gruff and feisty retired Marine Corps officer (rather stubborn and understandably so), who had been in charge of the local Toys for Tots program since the Stone Age. He wasn't about to give up his cherished role as the agency's annual Santa Claus. He dug in his heels like the Japanese he fought on Iwo Jima.

As news director, it became my mission to present this unusual and novel idea of cooperation and unity to him, and, as expected, it wasn't received well—not initially, anyway. All the other agencies fell in line without much hesitation.

Our goal soon having been achieved for the most part, it was then decided that all food, toys, and clothing gathered by all the nonprofits would be delivered and housed at Tellefsen's tiny Unity headquarters under the Victoria Theater, where the less fortunate folk throughout the community who qualified would enter her mini-warehouse to select the items they needed for their families and would leave with their dignity intact.

It was this very special part of the process that caught the attention of other actors, celebrities, and stars who lived in the area, and who would over the years very much desire to be a part of the annual fundraiser.

It was decided that an early weekend in December would be prime time for a live, televised event broadcast on Channel 3, starting in the afternoon and wailing its way into the late evening. KEYT's news anchors and reporters, side-by-side with local luminaries, would provide the pitch for money and present the various musical performances sprinkled throughout the merry marathon.

The studio was transformed into what may as well have been someone's giant living room, decked to the halls with a glowing fireplace right next to a huge decorated Douglas fir, with hundreds of colorful poinsettias interspersed among the hundreds of brightly wrapped presents in all shapes and sizes all around the room.

Any space left over was dedicated to a phone bank, manned by tireless volunteers who collected pledges from the thousands of callers who decided to donate.

The patio deck outside also was spruced up as a backdrop for all the singers who came to perform their holiday harmony.

Cameras were provided for the Hollywood hosts entrenched in the Unity Shoppe, and for our roving reporters traveling the streets in a live van capturing the spirit and generosity of people all over town.

It was a highly spirited scene, and quite a magical time.

Kenny Loggins, who had said he would just make an appearance, got so into the evening that he confiscated my microphone and wouldn't give it back for the rest of the night. I had to grab a stand-by to interview Santa Claus, who I recognized and saluted as soon as I saw him: that old Toys for Tots Marine had finally joined the party.

The first KEYT Christmas Unity Telethon in December of 1987 was so successful that many more would follow over the years, I'm proud to say.

I am blessed as well for being a part of its inception. It truly was a holy night—but silent, it was not.

[December 2014]

Downtown Miracles

The art of Christmas shopping as I remember it is not what it used to be.

Seems it was not too long ago—maybe it was—where in the days just before Christmas I'd see an avenue like Post Street in San Francisco come alive with couples, exhaling the cold night air, casually strolling by the endless and glittering displays of elegant storefronts. Or moms and dads with their animated children in tow merrily bobbing along the lane in great anticipation of meeting up with Santa Claus holding court in what used to be the White House department store.

For at least five consecutive years as we were growing up in the fifties, my brother and I, all decked out in the same little suits and the same little trench coats, paid a visit there just to perch on the knees of the jolly old man. I've got the pictures to prove it. Framed, of course.

As we grew older and the years went by, another family tradition was born, probably at the behest of my mom and encouraged by my older sister, whereby family members and friends would gather in the city for what would always turn out to be, come rain or shine, an adventurous day of gift seeking, highlighted by a rambunctious lunch at an eating establishment across Market Street called Breens, infamous at the time for having the longest and oldest wooden bar in San Francisco.

Needless to say that part of the seasonal joy we all experienced during this venerable occasion was no doubt enhanced by the time we all discovered it was late afternoon.

My personal favorite Christmas shopping expeditions occurred when my wife Sara and I were living in Santa Barbara, before a very serene downtown State Street was transformed into a land of corporate malls and madness.

Local shop owners and entrepreneurs didn't necessarily rule the roost, but there was definitely a hometown feeling about exchanges between proprietor and customer.

My plan was simple, and made much easier by the fact that Sara and I had no children to be concerned about. I never knew what she might have had in store for me; as for her, I'd wait until the final Saturday before Christmas day, and starting at about the location of the Arlington Theater, would walk down one side of State Street and up the other, entering each store to see what might catch my fancy for something she might appreciate as a Yuletide gift.

Never fearing that I'd come up empty or be forced to buy just anything so I wouldn't come home without, I had confidence that each and every store might offer something unusual or practical that I could have gift-wrapped.

My Saturday walk never failed, for several years, because the various and sundry businesses had all kinds of things to offer: everything from records (yes, records and tapes before the advent of CDs), books, knick-knacks, furniture, electronics, crafts and hobbies, to clothing, shoes, jewelry, and other apparel.

State Street was as rich as what was in Santa's bag, and the bargains were there if you either looked or haggled for them, which was something most of the storeowners loved to do back then.

Along the route I'd stop for coffee (pre-Starbucks) or a snack, and would almost always meet someone I knew, which made my trip all the more intriguing because we would exchange ideas as well as pleasantries.

My favorite stop ultimately turned out to be a most unusual store located in El Paseo (long before Paseo Nuevo) that traded in all kinds of disparate items, new and old, including a rather rare Native American bowl from somewhere in the Southwest, used to display things like beads and necklaces until I asked the shopkeeper specifically for the ancient crockery at a fair price.

Having discovered my prize of the day, I wrapped it up in a plain brown box once I got home, having convinced Sara that it was probably some kind of present like a Pendleton shirt from Uncle Charlie in the Pacific Northwest—the kind of gift you can appreciate but usually ends up being opened last, the perfect surprise for someone who is not expecting to unwrap a treasure crafted centuries ago.

It turned out I found three more of these bowls from the same shop on the next three years of my Christmas walks, until it finally closed. Each time it was from "Uncle Charlie," and each time Sara couldn't believe I found another plate or pottery from the past.

So if you're still searching for that special gift for a special loved one, and you haven't got much time, you can click the impersonal Internet, or brave the harried mall (neither of which offer much spirit), or you can take a leisurely walk this Saturday along the downtown streets of your choice.

Enjoy nog, engage a friend, and keep your eyes wide open and your spirits up.

You never know when you might end up finding something from Uncle Charlie under the Christmas tree.

[December 2011]

Carnival of the Animals

Some surprising things come your way when you are a news director and anchorman for television news, as it did for me in my waning years at KEYT in Santa Barbara.

In 1993, to my enchantment, and for reasons that are still a bit fuzzy, I was chosen by Bach Camerata to be narrator for the Ogden Nash version of French composer Camille Saint-Saëns's classic composition "Carnival of the Animals."

Adrian Spence, a flutist from Ireland and leader of the small chamber orchestra called at the time Bach Camerata (it is now known as Camerata Pacifica), invited me to narrate the piece for showings in Ventura at City Hall, in Santa Barbara at the Music Academy of the West, and at the Santa Barbara City Zoo for two concerts on Mother's Day in 1994 and 1995.

Composed by Saint-Saëns in 1886 and one of his best-liked suites, "Carnival of the Animals" is a delightful and highly spirited salute to our animal kingdom, and the instruments used reflect the temperament and sounds of the animals chosen.

The elephant is represented by double bass and piano and is marked *allegro pomposo*, the perfect caricature for an elephant. The piano plays a waltz-like triplet figure while the bass hums the melody beneath it. This is also a musical joke—the two themes were originally written for high, lighter-toned instruments; the joke is that Saint-Saëns moves this to the lowest and heaviest-sounding instrument in the orchestra, the double bass.

The 25-minute suite in 14 movements is fun, inventive, and light.

The narration between movements was penned by Ogden Nash in 1949, who wrote a set of humorous verses to accompany each movement, like the one for the "Fossils." Imagine being surrounded by some of the best classical musicians in the world as they stop for you to interpret this:

> *Amid the mastodontic wassail*
> *I caught the eye of one small fossil.*
> *"Cheer up, sad world," he said, and winked—*
> *"It's kind of fun to be extinct."*

I had so much fun with the experience that I memorized all my lines; I didn't want to read them so much as to talk them.

I have to say it was far more enjoyable than reading almost anything off a teleprompter.

I remember my mom, who was a classical music devotee, sending me a clipping from the LA Times promoting the 1995 performance at the Santa Barbara Zoo: "Joanne and Gavin Martin, a husband-and-wife piano duo, will be featured, with narration by King Harris of KEYT. Before the main concert, students of Santa Barbara's Music and Arts Conservatory will perform. There will also be a tribute to zoo animals that became mothers in the past year."

The zoo was the perfect place for a concert such as this.

With the sun shining, musicians shielded by a small tent on a grassy knoll filled with mothers and children, and real, live animals nearby, one couldn't ask for a better setting. Or a greater honor.

[June 2015]

Stormy Weather

Don't you just love it when all you hear months upon end is someone who complains, "Gee, I wish it would rain, we need it so badly," and that same person 24 hours later, following a sprinkle or two under abnormal Central Coast cloudy and gray skies, saying, "Rain, rain, rain. I'm so tired of this rain. If the sun doesn't come out, I'm going to go crazy."

I'd be the first to admit, having lived in Portland, Oregon, for five years, that constant damp and gloomy weather can indeed have a demoralizing effect on one's disposition.

But I am more than willing to put up with a nice storm or two, especially if they help replenish our water supply.

Besides, nothing makes me feel better than settling down in front of a fireplace with a good book during a steady rain.

However, I could do without the wind-driven tempest that causes widespread damage or destruction, no matter how much rain we need, because I know I'll be out in the midst of it, either as a news reporter covering floods and fallen trees or as a homeowner dealing with floods and fallen trees.

Take 1995, for example.

It's 4 o'clock in the morning during an unusual, very heavy, January rain. A shrill sound breaks the stillness, but it's not the alarm, it's the telephone.

"King, this is John. You better get to the TV station right away, or else you'll never make it." It was one of my reporters, John Palminteri, warning me that rising floodwaters were making Santa Barbara roads impassable and that some low-lying neighborhoods were already under siege.

I immediately rushed out of the house, but just before I got into my car to cross town, something told me to check the basement—it was raining that hard.

To my surprise and dismay, I found stored boxes and furniture floating in three feet of muddy water. But as news director for KEYT, and since there was nothing I could do at the moment and we weren't in any danger, I left my wife Sara behind to deal with our problem at home and faced the larger challenge of dealing with much of Santa Barbara being inundated by several feet of rising floodwaters.

Conditions got so bad throughout the day, the city became an island: you couldn't get in or out of Santa Barbara by air, boat, rail, or car.

Creeks turned into deadly, rampaging rivers. One man, a prominent judge, was torn from the desperate clutches of his wife as a torrent cascaded through their home in Strawberry Canyon, sending him a mile downstream where he was eventually discovered drowned and floating next to a bridge.

Hundreds of homes on the south side were accessible only by watercraft. Major and minor roadways were impassible.

Clogged underpasses literally turned into lakes, beckoning thrill-seekers to take the plunge on live TV, for which we got chastised. How dare you show such scenes—you're only inviting more trouble, viewers cried.

The skies eventually cleared and the waters receded, but the landscape was a muddy mess, including our basement, which fortunately had been pumped dry.

Believing the worst was over, and such a destructive wintertime event an anomaly, our news department nonetheless settled down to assess how we would cover such an emergency if it were ever to happen again.

We didn't have to wait long. A month later, and a week after a giant mudslide buried several homes in La Conchita, another winter storm parked itself off our coastline.

The weather forecast in the morning indicated that this latest tempest might reach San Luis Obispo but not Santa Barbara. At 7 o'clock that night, I started cursing the prediction. The rains came down so hard this time around that not only was our basement flooded for a second time, despite the new drains, but our garage was overcome as well.

To make matters worse, the power went out. I had to break out a window to get into the flooded cellar which now could not be pumped. It was while I was, to no avail, bailing water to save our cars that I got word from the station that not only was Santa Barbara getting deluged again, but parts of San Luis Obispo and Monterey counties were getting pummeled as well.

I'll never forget the image of a gas station sign atop a pole barely sticking above 13-plus feet of water in downtown Cambria, or aerial video of what once was a fertile Salinas Valley that resembled a swamp.

So as fond as I am of rain, and as much as we need it, I am hoping we get through the next several months without the kind of wicked winter weather that does more than fill our reservoirs, the kind that sends reporters out in parkas and rowboats, homeowners down to the basement or up to the roof, and emergency services down the proverbial pole.

That is, if the Lord is willing and the creek don't rise.

[January 2008]

Fire Now Fatal

It was a Thursday morning, June 28, 1990, the day after the wind-driven Painted Cave fire raced down a Santa Barbara mountainside vaporizing hundreds of homes and scorching thousands of acres in what seemed like a matter of minutes.

The property damage was inestimable. But the fire's furious flames would also take a life, as I was about to find out.

I was producing a special 6 a.m. news report for KEYT-TV. I had been up all night, reporting on the fire's fury, and later the destruction it left behind. At 5:30, the phone rang. It was long distance, from New York.

"Hello, can you help me?" It was a woman's voice, and she sounded terribly distraught.

"My daughter is missing," she continued. "I need to know if she's all right."

"Lady, a lot of people have been displaced," I impatiently replied. Then realizing how upset she was, I tried to calm her. "She's probably at a Red Cross center."

"No, no, you don't understand!" She was very persistent and determined. "Something has happened to her. I know it has. She calls me every single night, and last night she didn't call." She sounded unusually sure of herself.

"My daughter's name is Andrea Gurka. Her husband Michael just called me. He doesn't even know where she is."

She gave me her phone number and that of her son-in-law. I

reassured her, promised I would do some checking, and would call her back with any news. But her ominous tone didn't sit well with me.

After the broadcast, I called Michael Gurka, who, unable to go home, was staying at a friend's house in Goleta. He wasn't there, I was told. He was out looking for his wife. I alerted the Sheriff's Department and Red Cross, confident that once the smoke finally cleared, she would eventually turn up.

By Thursday evening, rumors were rampant about a woman whose whereabouts were unknown.

The next morning, our worst fears were realized. Andrea Gurka's body was found face down in a creek not far from her house in the woods directly in the path of the Wednesday night's inferno.

I called her mother, who had just been on the phone with the coroner's office. We spoke for an hour, about Andrea's dreams, hopes, and inspirations.

"You know it's ironic," I remember her telling me, calmly. "During the last conversation that my daughter and I had, she mentioned that when she died, she didn't want her body to be cremated."

I was to learn, in talking with Andrea's husband Michael, that his wife had suffocated. On the phone from his friends' house, Michael told me that when the fire first broke out, he was in Montecito finishing errands and heading home. He immediately called his wife and told her to leave. But how could she? Their neighbor was nowhere around. She couldn't drive out—the new battery to her car, one of Michael's errands, was in his trunk. And she couldn't walk out because she had a weak knee.

The only option, they both decided, was that she head for the creek and lie low in the water until he got there. But the fire denied him access. All he could do that Wednesday night was hope and pray that his wife had survived.

And that she might have done, fire investigators later told Michael, had she moved 10 yards to either side of where her body was found.

Michael knew, whether he liked it or not, that Andrea's death was now the top news story, and related to me that morning that he needed time to think about whether or not to appear on our news that evening. He called a half-hour before the newscast and said he had something to say.

I rushed out to his friend's house in Goleta to capture on tape what I could and then back to the studio to get it on the air.

I'll never forget first gazing upon the man who was suffering the loss of his dearest companion. Through the screen door between us, all I could see were his eyes, steadfastly penetrating through the screen's gauze.

In front of the camera, Michael very calmly and with assurance spoke for 40 seconds, not so much about the enormous tragedy of the now-deadly fire, but more about overcoming the losses shared in order to rebuild the community and re-kindle its spirit.

For a man I imagined was burdened with such grief and possible guilt, it was a very powerful and positive message.

We aired it moments later that night, and in the days that followed, Michael received the overwhelming support of the community. He appeared on our Painted Cave fire telethon a week later, not only as a volunteer answering the phones for donations for fire victims, but as a guest speaker throughout the evening, where his presence exposed the pain of the past yet provided an inspiration for the future.

I didn't see Michael for a year after that, when he called me on the first anniversary of the Painted Cave fire. We agreed I'd produce a follow-up story on his life since then.

I found him once again to be living in Santa Barbara's volatile backcountry. The weather was warm that afternoon, and a breeze was blowing. The wind chimes were clattering.

We looked at each other. He didn't have to say a word.

[July 2008]

You Be the Judge

I got a jury summons the other day. I get one every year, which puzzles me because news reporters like myself rarely make it to the jury box. We may know things about a case that other jurors don't, so we are more often than not excused. Why we are even considered for jury pool is beyond me.

I learned this the hard way when I was news director for KEYT television in Santa Barbara. It was 1985, and I was summoned to appear as a prospective juror in the country's first major legal battle against a tobacco company.

The case involved one John Galbraith of Goleta, who for 54 years chain-smoked cigarettes made by the R.J. Reynolds tobacco company, right up until the day he died at the age of 69 after suffering from lung cancer, emphysema, and heart disease. He was so addicted that he would remove the oxygen tubes from his nose so he could sneak a smoke.

When the notorious and flamboyant San Francisco attorney Melvin Belli, the self-proclaimed "King of Torts," got wind of this, he filed a $100 million lawsuit against RJR at the behest of Galbraith's former wife Elayne.

Before the trial even got started, it was a circus.

Opposing Belli, who came down to Santa Barbara in his yacht, was a defensive plethora of RJR corporate attorneys, public relations people, legal secretaries, and psychologists.

Selected to oversee this drama was a controversial judge by the name of Bruce Dodds, who would later be portrayed as one of America's worst magistrates on the ABC news show 20/20 because of his apparent intense dislike of women.

With a cast like this, and with a subject matter so controversial, media from all over the world descended upon sleepy Santa Barbara like the birds in the Hitchcock movie.

In the midst of all this was I, not only as a possible juror, but also as the reporter and anchor covering the story for the town's only TV station.

How could I do both, I asked the judge.

"You can be fair and impartial, can't you Mr. Harris?"

"Of course, your Honor, but I feel there is a conflict of interest here," I replied.

It was the wrong answer.

"Sit down and wait to be called, Mr. Harris."

So that's what I did, for more than a week. Out of more than 250 prospective jurors, I was the last one to be called. And I came to find out that decision was deliberate.

Judge Dodds had been informed by one of RJR's "spies" that I was overheard early on discreetly exchanging background and statistical information about the case with one of my reporters, who unbeknownst to both of us happened to be standing right next to a possible jurist. No order had yet been given not to say anything, so I continued reporting.

Dodds had other ideas. He hauled me into his chambers with the attorneys from both sides, and accused me of tainting the mind of a prospective juror, causing her dismissal and thereby holding up the proceedings.

"I did not talk with this woman, your Honor."

"It is my understanding that she overheard you."

"Did she tell you that?" I asked.

"No. Someone else did, Mr. Harris."

"Who?"

"That's none of your concern, Mr. Harris. Go back into the court-room and wait to be called."

A reporter from another TV station later told me that one of RJR's secretaries had been shadowing me and planted herself right next to me while I had been conversing with my colleague. I was surprised I wasn't given the boot as well, considering, but my punishment would come later. Much later.

After all the prospective jurors went through the ordeal of initial questioning, I was finally called and then promptly told I was excused. So I watched the drama unfold from a seat in the courtroom as opposed to one on the jury panel.

The trial lasted five weeks. Belli tried to convince the jury that his deceased client was truly addicted to nicotine and couldn't help himself. RJR countered that it was Galbraith's responsibility.

Despite all the current and growing negativity towards smoking, including the pronouncements of then-Surgeon General Dr. C. Everett Koop, Belli failed to garner the popular support he was expecting. The jury was not convinced that Galbraith was indeed addicted, or that smoking killed him. It voted 9-3 in favor of acquittal.

The circus was over, but I could have done without the clowns.

[August 2007]

Feud and Folly

"Extra! Extra! Read all about it!"

There was a time last century when kids wearing cocked hats with newspapers in hand would cry out and hawk the dailies of the day from street corners and newsstands in major cities across America.

No longer, sadly, but if that era were to return, the same kids on the street corners of Santa Barbara trying to sell the Santa Barbara News-Press would most likely be hollering, "Extra! Extra! Read all about nothing!"

That's because, many locals believe, Wendy McCaw, the owner and co-publisher of the News-Press, has turned one of California's oldest and most respected daily newspapers literally into a rag.

The story of her tumultuous tenure has been chronicled by some Santa Barbara filmmakers in an illuminating documentary entitled *Citizen McCaw* (with a facetious nod to Orson Welles), which premiered in a Friday-night showing two weeks ago at the Arlington Theater in downtown Santa Barbara.

McCaw, divorced and rich as Croesus, was seen as a savior when she bought the News-Press in 2000 from the corporate New York Times. But the expected locally-owned direction and flavor evaporated about a year-and-a-half ago when a group of newspaper staffers, including editors, reporters, and columnists, some with multiple years of popular position, were either fired or quit.

Since that time, the number has grown close to 80, and many of those have been maligned, slandered, or sued by an owner who many people (including much of the town's citizenry) say is malicious, vindictive, and arrogant, not to mention irresponsible, journalistically unethical, and oppressive. Charges she vehemently denies.

Attorneys for the reclusive McCaw, who was asked but declined to be in the film, claim she has the right to do anything she wants to with her newspaper, including how and what news is covered. And that's exactly what she did when she took over the publishing reins with her fiancé and bon vivant Arthur von Wiesenberger in 2006.

When one scribe reported on the DUI sentencing of the paper's editorial page editor, the story was quashed.

When another reported the address of actor Rob Lowe, who was embroiled in a building controversy on his Montecito property in an issue open to the public, the reporter was sternly admonished. Lowe had called McCaw to complain. McCaw then asserted it was terrible judgment on the part of the news department.

It was incidents such as these that drove news editor Jerry Roberts and other popular newsroom personnel to resign, and others would follow. Those news employees who did remain publicly demonstrated their own grievances outside the News-Press building in De La Guerra Plaza; once, claiming they were being silenced, they covered their mouths with duct tape.

There were also many protests staged by influential townspeople and government leaders, who lamented McCaw's alleged violation of the public trust leading to what they perceived to be the destruction of the paper's credibility and reputation.

And while news staffers were gathering votes to bring a union into the picture, McCaw sued Roberts and implied that he had downloaded child pornography on his newsroom computer. Roberts was never contacted for his response to the allegations that made front page news in McCaw's newspaper.

McCaw has other lawsuits pending against other newspapers and publications, and though she just lost one ordering her to reinstate several newsroom employees, she plans to appeal.

The heiress certainly doesn't show any signs of giving up, or giving in, which may have tragic consequences for the community, according to renowned journalists—locals Sander Vanocur and Lou Cannon, and former Washington Post executive editor Ben Bradlee—who appear in the film. The wall between news and editorial has come tumbling down, they agree, and news must not succumb to that kind of interference.

It's been my experience that Wendy McCaw won't be the first or last owner of a media property to exert influence on the news it either prints or broadcasts. I have worked under several whose self-interest, ego, and greed have superseded or interfered with the responsibility and purpose of gathering and reporting the news the public needs to know.

So after seeing *Citizen McCaw* at the Arlington, I had great respect for the 30 or so former employees of the Santa Barbara News-Press who gathered onstage after the film to take their bows to thunderous applause from an audience who appreciated as much as I did their courage to stand up for what they believe.

We're all better for it.

[March 2008]

9

San Luis Obispo

Give credit to the people of San Luis Obispo County, who rose up by way of letter, email, and phone call to such an extent that it prompted a re-examination of the situation and re-consideration of abandoning the "news" in KVEC "news-talk." It was soon realized how special and closely-knit this community is, which of course is what makes it so unique and distinctive.

~ Power to the People

King Harris
News Anchor
1998-2001, 2006-2015

Birth of a Station

The year is 1937.

The Spanish Civil War is raging. The Japanese invade China. Adolph and his Nazis control Germany. President Roosevelt is elected for the second time. Amelia Earhart disappears over the Pacific. The Golden Gate Bridge spans the bay. Newsweek magazine is published. Bugs Bunny and Snow White make their film debuts. Spam and Kix are launched. Robert Redford, Jack Nicholson and Dustin Hoffman are born.

The year 1937 also gave birth to KVEC, San Luis Obispo's first radio station, which started broadcasting on May 8.

Legend has it that one Christine Jacobson, who, along with one George Frederick Muff, both owners of an appliance store called the Valley Electric Company, aligned themselves with one Les Hacker, just out of the Merchant Marines with an interest in radio broadcasting. So 'VEC' was attached to a 'K' and KVEC was created.

News of the debut made the Daily Telegram front page underneath a picture of the burning dirigible Hindenburg (which crashed in Lakehurst, New Jersey, two days earlier) and the headline "Airship Death Toll Swells to 35; Inquiries Continue."

The article reported that "San Luis Obispo's long-awaited radio station KVEC officially went on the air at 7 a.m. Saturday for its regular schedule of broadcasts. The station's wavelength is 1200 kilocycles, power 250 watts, and it will be on the air daily from 7 a.m. to 7 p.m. A special three-hour broadcast Monday evening from 8 to 11 p.m. will be put on the air from The Monday Club. A program of entertainment, with guest speakers from all sections of the county, is planned. Appropriate Mother's Day music throughout Sunday has been programmed."

Since that very first day, through several ownership changes and through several hundred radio newspeople, entertainers, and personalities, KVEC at one time or another has broadcast nearly every conceivable kind of live and/or transcribed programming, local and otherwise: music and musical events, news, disasters, accident reports, road conditions, farm reports, stock market quotations, weather, frost warnings, ski conditions, sports, Dodger baseball and Ram, Bruin, Mustang and Tiger football, public service announcements, meeting notices, bulletin boards, club news, church news, employment opportunities, editorials, and of course the live talk format that has its roots in a program called *The Party Line* in 1956 and continues to this day with hometown radio host Dave Congalton, whose debut in 1992 was somewhat auspicious in that it was delayed because lightning struck the transmitter tower.

The thunder, however, has yet to stop.

In 1937 and for several years following, KVEC's studio and transmitter were located at the same site, on the hill above Cal Poly near Highland and Highway 101.

In 1955, the studio was moved to Hill Street, just one of the many locations it was to have. On Christmas Eve of that year, the transmitter caught fire and was destroyed. KVEC was off the air for only five days, however, because in four days RCA had shipped the necessary equipment from the East Coast to Los Angeles, where in one day Les Hacker picked it up in his truck and installed it overnight.

It was during this time that KVEC-TV was also in operation. After three years, KVEC-TV became KSBY-TV in 1956.

Over the years, KVEC 920 AM has produced a plethora of many behind-the-mike notables, including Les Hacker, Chuck Cecil, Bill Barton, Russ James, Frank Potter, Fred Peterson, Alan Ross, Dan Clarkson, Dave Cox, Bill Benica, Suzan Vaughn, Scott Roarke, and Paul Kelly, to name a few that I'm familiar with.

I joined this illustrious group in 1999, when I was appointed news director while insurance man Frank Sheahan owned and operated KVEC on Chorro Street.

What a stint that was. OK, so I didn't have to climb a 264-foot tower to replace one of the seven light bulbs like they did in the past, but the future had yet to arrive. Tape was still the medium of the day, as were machines that sometimes refused to play it.

When Clear Channel bought KVEC in 2000, they moved the studio to Zaca Lane and propelled the station into communication's computer age.

After a brief hiatus, I returned as morning news anchor to find that the radio station's purpose hadn't changed all that much since the day of its first broadcast 70 years ago: to provide a local voice for local people.

[May 2007]

Christmas in SLO

Christmas is a wonderful and wacky time in San Luis Obispo.

It's a time when, before the Thanksgiving turkey is even out of the oven and despite our warm winter weather, Jack Frost is nipping at your nose...and ears.

At least two local radio stations, COAST 101.3 and K-JEWEL 1400, start spinning the proverbial Yuletide favorites 24 hours a day. And if you miss "White Christmas" on the radio, you're sure to hear it in shopping centers where retailers hope that Der Bingle's dream will induce you to part with your money.

It's a time when downtown San Luis Obispo turns into a wonderland, with this year's 31st annual Christmas parade, featuring 100 highly spirited entries, proceeding down a crowded and colorful Higuera Street lined with children of all ages.

It's a time when Mission Plaza takes on the appearance of the North Pole; when empty lots and parking spots suddenly sprout Douglas firs and Ponderosa pines; when mistletoe and holly deck the halls and eave-laden icicles light up the nights; when local espresso houses serve up eggnog lattes and other Christmas cheer in bright-colored holiday mugs; when chimney sweeps clear the way for Santa (although some won't admit it).

It's also a time when our local police department pulls you over to award you a turkey for good driving, and our meter readers present you with you a parking pass instead of a parking ticket.

And of course it wouldn't be Christmas without Madonna's towering tree that sits atop Cerro San Luis providing a beacon for us all.

At least, that's how Phyllis Madonna describes it. She along with her husband Alex put it there many seasons ago.

"Alex and I always felt wonderful about the top of that mountain," she told me. "We used to just climb it periodically, just for the fun of it. You get to the top of that mountain and it's just magical. In 1980, I gave a birthday party for Alex up there, where we built a stage, which is still there.

"One Christmas we had a local church that wanted to go up there with their choir and they wanted to sing under the tree we had put up a couple of years before. The church choir proceeded to sing Christmas carols and I felt after reading some of the letters we had received that our Christmas tree represented hope and peace for the community."

Never lacking in spirit, Christmas or otherwise, Alex Madonna once assured me during an electrical brownout several years ago that his tree would be lit no matter what: he always used his own generator, and it's been generating goodwill ever since. At least Phyllis thinks so.

And about silent nights and first Noels, Phyllis added, "I'm just very sentimental, and so was Alex."

Of the many stories about the Madonna tree, one in particular stands out.

"We got a call once from a lady at the bottom of the mountain who was taking care of a young man whose wife and child were recently killed in an auto accident," Phyllis said. "Doctors told him he would never be able to walk again. He promised himself that he would, and that by the next Christmas he would walk to the top of the mountain where that tree was. It was sort of like a beacon of light, a beacon of hope. And believe it or not, that young man made it to the top."

According to Phyllis, she and Alex both loved Christmas and that tree. "It looks like it's hanging in mid-air. Everything around it is dark. It's like it's coming from heaven."

Christmas is a wonderful and wacky time in San Luis Obispo.

[December 2006]

Little Drummer Boy

"Don't do it—you'll never make it," advised a boss I used to have.

He owned a radio station in the Portland, Oregon area and I was selling airtime. I had just told him about my friend Bill Schwartz, a singer-songwriter who needed a drummer for a rock group he was putting together with plans to make it big in Los Angeles. Since I had the chops for such a gig, having drummed through college in a rock 'n' roll band, I decided, against any prevailing wisdom, to join up and head south.

"Okay," my boss said, a little miffed I think because I was leaving. "But you aren't going to make it." He ended up being right, which miffed me a little bit.

It was hard to break into the musical scene in the early 1970s, despite some pretty decent recordings we made in Portland, San Francisco, and Los Angeles. Besides, Bill, playing in a crude style similar to that of a more polished Elton John, wasn't trying to sell the group as much as he was his songs. He had the contract with A&M Records—we didn't— and consequently the band broke up.

I survived the ordeal by drumming for various groups, playing mostly in clubs and bars, where alcohol seemed to be the reigning customer. Think of Billy Joel's "Piano Man" and you get the idea.

Bill Schwartz sold a few tunes and died trying. The crazy LA rock scene put him in his youthful grave, and that's when I decided to hang up my sticks, sell my drums, and get back into broadcasting.

I think of those years every time I drive by the Drum Circuit on Higuera Street in San Luis Obispo. Once in a while I get the urge to go into the place to check out what is new in the drumming world, but I doubt I'll ever see a trap set in my living room anytime soon.

But who knows? After talking with Steve Hilstein the other day, I might change my mind. Hilstein owned the Drum Circuit for nearly 20 years before he sold it to a friend not long ago. He still teaches his Drum School 101 there, however, and stays connected to the business.

What has always intrigued me about the Drum Circuit, certainly one of the more highly visible landmarks in San Luis Obispo, is how they have managed to stay in business. I mean, how many drummers are there on the Central Coast? Enough to support two legendary drum shops, apparently—the other being in Santa Barbara.

Hilstein credits his love of pounding the skins and teaching his students. "I started playing 43 years ago when I was 10. I still have the record that inspired me. It was 'Rock Around the Clock' by Bill Haley and the Comets. Whatever the drummer was doing, I was hooked! I remember making a drum set out of Quaker Oats cereal boxes when I was nine."

Then Hilstein got serious.

"I started playing for a living when I was 18, and when I turned 25 and moved here, I made a decision in my life, and it was a turning point.

"Is this something I'm going to do as a career, or should I get a real job? Obviously I kept going and began studying seriously with an instructor. Later on I went to a percussion school in Hollywood called P.I.T.—the Percussion Institute of Technology—the trade school for drummers."

Hilstein says he learned a lot, and was now equipped with the skills to teach. On top of that, he got a resale license and opened up the Drum Circuit. "I love to play drums and teach drums. I love the results I see in students' lives. It's something I can share with them because it turns their lives around."

While he's not teaching, Hilstein is busy with a novel approach to percussion he created called the Bucket Busters.

"We use anything we can beat on not made by manufacturers, like different sizes of metal trash cans, or five-gallon plastic buckets, or various sizes of empty water bottles. Every Saturday 10 or 12 of us drummers will get together and produce an extraordinary sound. We play all over—in parades, Farmers Markets, and charitable events."

Hilstein is also responsible for an annual highly successful drum competition, where every year 26 contestants in two different age categories get together to show off their individual skills. His twentieth was just held last weekend at the Graduate. "It benefits the San Luis Obispo Child Abuse Prevention Council, so it's a win-win event for everybody." Hilstein advises that if you enter, it pays to be more versatile.

If you love all types of musical styles, he says, you can actually make a living playing drums. Short of that, follow your heart, even if you never drum the big time.

[April 2009]

It's What's in the Groove That Counts

Imagine my surprise and shock when I walked up to Boo Boo Records in Grover Beach and instead of seeing the usual concert posters adorning the entrance, I ran into giant sheets of blank white paper hugging the storefront windows, a locked door, and a small sign expressing regret that the store had suddenly closed. It referred customers to the flagship operation in downtown San Luis Obispo.

I thought my favorite music store had gone under. I was saddened but relieved at the same time. It doesn't sit well with me when record stores close down.

I grew up inhaling rock 'n' roll and pop music. In the '50s, a transistor radio was my closest companion, and Joe Prein's record store was my home away from home. Singles—45 RPM records, the ones with the big holes—were the play of the day, and I remember spending hours listening to them on Joe's specially equipped turntables in one of his three listening booths.

I can't say if it weren't for me Joe would have gone out of business a lot earlier than he did, but I ended up buying most of the records I played there, many of which I still have to this day (much to my wife's chagrin).

Real music stores, whether they sell vinyl, compact discs, DVDs or tapes, should offer an emotional experience. Owners like Mike White of Boo Boo Records understand this. It's been his life's blood.

When White first came to Cal Poly in 1974, Brown's Record store on Higuera was on the wane. Boo Boo's was soon to become a hipper alternative.

"Like any other kid who loved music, I was in Boo Boo's almost since the first day they opened up by the train station," White said. "I was in there almost every day, to the point where then-owners Ed Taylor and Glen Forbes thought I should be behind the counter."

Although White majored in ornamental horticulture, seeds of his future had already been planted in another landscape. When Boo Boo's moved downtown in 1978, White became manager of that store, but oversaw operations in the Grover Beach location as well.

"The record industry was a goldmine back then," he recalls. "You were the only game in town as a store. You were the keepers of the key."

White and Boo Boo's also cared about the needs and desires of their customers, probably the chief reason for their success. They provided not only selection but service, and started to develop a following they have to this day.

"We're lucky," White says. "We have a really loyal clientele. It's saved us in a lot of ways."

It couldn't save the Grover Beach store, however. Shrinking compact disc sales overall and shrinking traffic at the location sealed its fate.

"We are no longer keeper of the key," White admits. "There's a variety of ways you can have music delivered now—Internet downloads, your friends burning CDs—that's fine, but the genie is not going back into the bottle."

Boo Boo's (so named because it was easy for its creator to remember under the spell of euphoria at the time) may have to undergo a lifestyle change to remain competitive in an age where more and more people are downloading their music from the Internet, or buying their CDs from non-music stores like Best Buy or Wal-Mart.

"We've always tried to keep our house in order," White asserts. "We always felt this is the best store with the best buy and deepest selection. Our store helps you find the music you want. We carry stuff based on our love for music, not based on someone giving money to place their CD in a store."

White and his partner John Hoffman bought Boo Boo Records from the original owners, and despite losing Grover, White is more optimistic than ever.

"Our online business is really the growth sector for Boo Boo Records. That's kind of our new second store. We see a lot of blue sky there."

[June 2007]

The Missing Link

One of the unfathomable riddles of my childhood revolved around the two bicycles I rode around on, both quite different but with one thing in common.

My first bike had no bells or whistles, only one speed, with the pedal for a brake. Later on, when I got an afternoon paper route for the Redwood City Tribune, I convinced my parents it might be difficult for me to negotiate the uphill curves and corners in the countryside without an upgrade, so they were kind enough to get me a Schwinn knockoff with a Sturmey-Archer three-speed (that I could conveniently shift while I was stopped), fenders, a kickstand, and a chain guard so I would no longer get grease on my trousers (a real selling point to my mom).

My new bike even came with a tire pump. My problem with both bikes was the crossbar, an item not featured on girl's bikes. For us boys, straddling the crossbar, by being where it was, could and often did cause considerable pain whenever our bikes suddenly stopped and we didn't. Future generations were being imperiled, I cried, every time I ran off the road into a ditch. But I was not about to ride around on a girl's bike for the sake of solving a problem.

So I wasn't too unhappy when I turned old enough to drive.

But these days the thought of a bicycle in my future is growing on me, especially after talking with some local folks about the adventurous plans for a continual bike path that will connect Cal Poly to Avila Beach in the not-so-distant future. What a fun ride. Also practical.

Two basic projects are being worked on: the Bob Jones City to the Sea Trail from Avila to San Luis Obispo, and the Railroad Safety Bicycle Trail from Cal Poly to SLO.

Jamie Hill, who represents Rideshare with the San Luis Obispo Council of Governments, told me that one day you'll be able to ride your bike from Mustang Stadium along the railroad tracks over Highway 101 to Marsh Street, then beyond to the Amtrak Station, down to Orcutt Road, then on to Tank Farm. This route will eventually connect to the Bob Jones Trail, which is working its way from the beach to Highway 101 to points north towards the city.

While most sections of the Railroad Safety Trail have been funded, one that has not is being called the "missing link," a 500-foot stretch from Campus Way to Foothill Boulevard.

Jan Howell Marx, representing San Luis Obispo Rotary, says this critical connection is too small to interest grant-giving agencies and too expensive for the city to fund by itself, which is why she tells me that Rotary recently donated $50,000 to pay for the safety fencing that parallels the bike trail. But that's only a part of the $307,000 needed.

So Marx is asking local residents to make a contribution. "Cal Poly is building new dorms, which means additional students, traffic, and congestion. It just makes sense for them to be able to get to and from San Luis Obispo by biking or walking instead of using a car."

Obviously it's also better for the environment. Marx says over 28,000 Rotary Clubs worldwide have designated an annual "Clean and Green" project to help the environment, so SLO Rotary has chosen to make the "missing link" is first beneficiary. "With the rising price of gas and climate change, any trip by bike or foot is a plus for the environment. It's also healthy for the person making that transportation decision."

Marx adds that travel by bike into San Luis Obispo wouldn't take all that much longer than travel by car—about 15-20 minutes, especially when you consider the problems of parking.

Rotary and other community sponsors hope to see the "missing link" completed sometime next year. Rotary President Roxanne Carr loves the idea of not having to use a car. "It is exciting for our Rotary Club to be leading a diverse coalition to raise funds for the Railroad

Safety Bicycle Trail. We are helping bring our city into the forefront of alternate transportation."

The "missing link" campaign is a three-month affair that started this May, which is also incidentally Bike Month, a period during which an all-out effort will be made to get more people like me onto bicycles.

No one knows for sure when the bike-only routes will be finished, but when it is, please give me some room.

It's been a long time since I traveled by bicycle, but the very idea that I will eventually be able to get from San Luis Obispo to the beach on a pathway without cars just might prompt me to dust off my old three-speed.

[May 2008]

The Perfect Storm

As you've probably heard by now, PG&E meteorologist John Lindsay has been reinstated, for which I and a lot of other people on the Central Coast are quite grateful.

He didn't get his old job back, but will be offering weather information to all who need or desire it as part of his duties in his new position as corporate relations representative for the company working out of the Diablo Canyon Power Plant.

John was one of many PG&E employees laid off several weeks ago as part of a restructuring plan at the plant to save the company money. What corporate execs weren't counting on was all the negative feedback they would get.

And they got an earful, most noticeably from my KVEC colleague Dave Congalton, who, upon hearing the news, raised such a stink on his afternoon talk show that even if PG&E CEO Peter Darbee had deaf ears he would have heard about it. And as soon as he did, wheels were set in motion to correct an unfortunate blunder.

The company's immediate response to John's departure, initially "Diablo Canyon can get its weather from other sources," changed within days to "We could have handled it better," a statement offered by PG&E's government liaison Pat Mullen, who added, "It was a good chance for us to learn. It was in PG&E's best interest to keep him."

That said, John will now be working in the communications department overseen by public information officer Pete Resler, who told me, "John will be doing one hundred percent community relations work. He will continue to do his weather reports. In addition to that, he will be speaking to schools about the power plant, PG&E, and the weather, if that's what people want to hear about."

Wait. There's more.

"John is also going to help us with plant tours and really spearheading our efforts to be more active in the community, including identifying and organizing volunteer events for our employees in local projects, and events like fairs and parades."

John Lindsay: from meteorologist to grand marshall. That's funny. That's what John was—an ambassador—before he was relieved. Resler had to find it out the hard way.

"As we heard from many in the community over the last couple of weeks, John's a very well respected and valued public servant. His weather reports were useful to a lot of people in the community, and we certainly heard from them."

Give credit to PG&E for listening. Most corporate entities wouldn't have bothered. Nuclear fusion, as it were, was eventually achieved.

"As I sat and thought about the needs in my group, I had two vacant positions," Resler said. "So John really was a perfect fit for one of those. John is really going to be able to spend all of his time doing what he loves to do and what he's really good at. I needed somebody with his skills and abilities, and the weather is the bonus."

John Lindsay is taking the whole thing in modest and humble John Lindsay-style and stride.

"I'm doing a lot better, that's for sure. It's great to be employed again, of course. But you know, King, here's the thing: being laid off is bad, there's no way to sugarcoat it of course, but there are a lot worse things that are happening to folks than like being just laid off from your job. One just has to look at the front page of the newspaper to see how fortunate we are, with everything else going on."

What was his initial reaction to the new deal?

"I was very surprised. I'll be doing weather, looking into increasing our wave forecasting abilities. The other part will be community outreach where I go out to schools to talk about science, energy, oceanography, and weather. I'll be doing a lot of community service and organizing events."

No doubt John's biggest support came from his family, especially his wife Trish, who weathered the storm with a low-pressure system.

"I never realized the importance of having Trish standing by my side, somebody I could lean on, because you know, King, it is difficult, and to have somebody there for me the way she supported me, I'll never forget that for the rest of my life," John said. "That, to me, was a great life lesson: that you have somebody you can lean on, and she came through with flying colors."

[October 2007]

Leaving the Broadcast Biz

I was startled, saddened, and disappointed upon learning last week of the impending departure of KSBY news anchor Jeanette Trompeter, who, after having co-anchored the Channel 6 desk since 2010, plans to leave next March.

So I called her up and told her how bummed I was to hear the news of her leaving, and to wish her well. She mentioned to me that her on-air hours on the weeknights were getting to be a bit much. I can relate, having anchored KMST in Monterey and KEYT in Santa Barbara for a total of 20 years.

It may seem like it, but it isn't easy being an anchor. All that primping and prepping might be perceived as being trivial, but when your job includes reporting and writing, it can become laborious. No matter why Jeanette is departing, I will miss her for a variety of reasons, not the least of which is her personable and likeable style, plus her experience. And the quality of her voice, which I think is important.

It's easy to get attached to such a presence, which makes it difficult to accept that soon she will no longer be in our living rooms every weeknight. When she does finally retire, she will join the ranks of some illustrious former KSBY co-anchors, who instead of moving on, decided to find new jobs in other arenas to remain in SLO County.

I discovered this in 2006 when I wrote a story for New Times called "Anchors Away." And the trend apparently continues. Since that article was written, former KSBY anchor and news director Tony Cipolla left his post and joined the SLO County Sheriff's Department as public information officer.

Others who preceded Tony in their separate quests: the legendary Rick Martell (now deceased), Missie Pires Hobson (now deceased), John Summer, Lynn Diehl, Jennifer Mandulay, Marcy Degarimore Eberle, Wendy Thies, Jill Ricket Talley, Jennifer Goss Plumber, Mitch Massey, Dave Garth, and Jim Byrne and Megan Maloney (from KCOY).

When I interviewed Rick in 2006, he told me, "I never wanted to pursue a singing career after I found out what it was all about. So I went to radio school. Believe it or not, I had a high squeaky voice back then and I didn't think I'd make it until I discovered the head of the broadcasting school had even a higher voice than mine." As for staying here after anchoring KSBY and KCOY newscasts: "In my semi-retirement years I never wanted to go to a bigger market. My granddaughter was here. Plus where else is there, really? God, this place is just wonderful."

That last refrain was pretty much echoed by just about everyone I talked to. Missie Hobson left on her own terms, and after spending three years with KSBY co-anchoring with Rick Martel, she took a job with PG&E. "PG&E offered a great 23 years with the company," she told me. "It was a tough decision at the time because I really liked reporting. But the salary and stability was difficult."

John Summer told me, "If I were to stay in broadcasting, I would have had to go to a bigger market. I didn't want to do that so decided to change professions so Liz and I could stay here."

Jennifer Mandulay summed it up this way: "I put my family first. In the broadcasting business it's difficult to raise a family."

Marci Degarimore told me nine years ago the reason she left KCOY was because the drive from Atascadero to Santa Maria was getting too tedious and dangerous. So she left and eventually married vintner Gary Eberle.

So keep the faith, Jeanette. You'll be in good company, and will soon understand, if you haven't already, that there's more to life than being a TV news anchor. A toast for all you've done.

[October 2015]

Power to the People

Thursday, December 13, 9:30 a.m. A call comes into the KVEC newsroom, confirming what we are hearing on the scanner: something is going on at Prado Road and South Higuera in San Luis Obispo.

All kinds of police and sheriff's deputies are running around with rifles and shotguns, closing down bi-ways and redirecting traffic. Prado itself from Higuera to the 101 freeway is closed, filled with local militia and dozens of police vehicles.

When I get to the scene with my tape recorder in hand, I am told by police spokesman Captain Dan Blanke that a car possibly involved with a bank robbery in LA met up with two other cars, and the people inside all three were being questioned. KVEC had it on the air within 30 minutes.

No question that it was newsworthy—a major arterial to Highway 101 was closed, and police were conducting an operation possibly involving federal crimes like bank robbery, including some in our area.

Later on, we find out police arrested eight suspects, seven of whom were booked on charges of conspiring to commit robbery. While not as tragic as the fatal shootings at Denny's, or as life-threatening as the Highway 41 fire, or as damaging as the San Simeon earthquake, or as disrupting as an overturned tanker blocking traffic during a morning commute, it is breaking news nonetheless.

One thing I learned about covering disasters live—the Painted Cave fire in Santa Barbara comes to mind—is that it is just as important (if not more so) to have a presence as it is to be giving out information.

That's just one of the reasons KVEC news exists: to be there, to inform the public not just what's going on during an emergency but to cover and deliver local news and information to Central Coast residents who need and deserve to know what's going on in their communities.

Whether the news involves government, political issues, education, crime, growth, real estate, business, health, lifestyle, weather, traffic, fundraising causes, sports, or arts and entertainment, local news is what KVEC has been providing for 70 years now, and thanks to the generous and overwhelming support of the community the past several weeks, local news is what KVEC will continue to provide.

Give credit to Clear Channel's successor, El Dorado Broadcasters, for not only hearing your voice but responding to it. When new owners of a broadcast entity take over, more often than not some changes are made (in this case, KVEC's morning news was replaced by a conservative syndicated talk show on November 30), and when they are, resistance is almost always expected. But then it usually diminishes.

Give credit to the people of San Luis Obispo County, who rose up by way of letter, email, and phone call to such an extent that it prompted a re-examination of the situation and re-consideration of abandoning the "news" in KVEC "news-talk." It was soon realized how special and closely-knit this community is, which of course is what makes it so unique and distinctive.

One of the reasons I never opted to progress to major markets throughout my career is because I got much more satisfaction getting involved with the individual rather than the masses. It's a position that a lot of journalists live for.

You become part of the community, you learn about its culture and its history, and you get to know its geography and its nuances, all the things that make it so exceptional.

You get to see the results of your efforts by getting immediate and personal feedback—your message isn't lost on a sea of souls.

Give credit to all those KVEC reporters and personalities over the years who helped establish, maintain, and further the station's news credibility and identity, and its accessibility to the listener.

Give credit to all the previous owners of KVEC throughout the years for keeping the station alive and vibrant, especially through many financially challenging and difficult times.

It's not an easy thing to accomplish, especially in this news media day and age where listeners, viewers, and readers are finding alternative ways of getting information they need when they want it. Given this, you might think the days of traditional news delivery are numbered: after all, it's no secret that newspaper readership is down, network TV news is losing viewers, and radio offers mostly opinion, not news. Competition for the ad dollar is tougher than ever.

As dire as this appears, all is not lost, as I have discovered during the past two tumultuous weeks.

Perhaps my colleague and good friend Dave Congalton, KVEC's local radio talk show host for the past 15 years, sums it up best on his show every weekday:

"Thank you for supporting KVEC, your hometown radio station."

[December 2007]

A Testament to Inspiration

No news is good news, they say, unless of course you read SLO City News.

The first edition of the bi-weekly publication, which made its debut August 11, 2006, was darn near a testament to inspiration. For example, there was an uplifting story of a woman whose children were almost killed in an accident, who were saved by the quick-thinking actions of a man she never met and probably never will. And did you see that color picture of four kids inhaling ice cream cones on the front page? Now there was a refreshing kind of scoop; it not only prompted me to search for the nearest sorbet shoppe, it almost prompted me to have children.

Other pages were filled with upbeat stories reflective of a positive community always in pursuit of ways to overcome the challenges that often present themselves in a paradise like ours. And many of those issues, I am told, will be addressed in forthcoming issues as well.

The man responsible for this daring affair is my friend and fellow journalism colleague Christopher Gardner, for whom I have somewhat of a sneaky admiration because he set out to do what he said he was going to do not quite three months ago amidst the groans of skeptical nay-sayers who always find ways to cast doubt on the possible success of another community-oriented print enterprise that might subvert the status quo.

To which I say: the more, the merrier. But then I happen to prefer all kinds of information from all kinds of different sources. And I appreciate the competitive spirit it fosters.

I don't get a driveway version of SLO City News because I don't reside within the city limits, but since what is happening in San Luis Obispo often affects nearby cities and towns, I made the effort to find a copy, just to see what Chris and company were up to.

Walk into their office on Broad Street and you'll meet a small, young, eager and energetic staff anxious to take on a new world, and an editor who hasn't slept much in a couple of months—pretty much what you might expect from a start-up.

I got the feeling before I even picked up the first copy of SLO City News that it would be the kind of paper that might chronicle people you've always seen but never met, or places you've yet to visit or experience.

If it is successful, and I see few reasons why it shouldn't be, it's going to be because its goal—one of them, anyway—is that it be accessible, inviting all kinds of tales to be told, a real people paper that is willing to offer those local stories, perspectives, observations, personalities, and news that often go unnoticed.

I'll bet my great-great-grandfather would appreciate an effort such as this. His name was James King of William (he tacked on William to differentiate himself from all the other Kings at the time). He started the Evening Bulletin (later the Call-Bulletin) in San Francisco in late 1855, mainly to flush out all the rapscallions, charlatans, and thieves among many of those in power at the time. It was virtually a one-man crusade until the local populace started to support his efforts.

As a former banker in the city and having lost his fortune in the financial panic of 1854-55, James King of William knew that the criminal element was closely tied to those with wealth who profited from political corruption. His was an undertaking not without danger—King's office was vandalized constantly, and he was forced to carry a gun.

In 1856 he went after a city supervisor named James Casey, who was trying to protect one Charles Cora, a notorious gambler who had gunned down and murdered a local marshal. King's attacks on the two were relentless, which caused Casey to shoot King in broad daylight outside his office near Montgomery Street, and while King lay dying for the next two days, the city's first vigilante committee was formed.

King died on May 22, 1856. Two days later, the vigilantes hanged both Casey and Cora. Eventually, because of all this, the city was cleaned up.

Now I am not suggesting that SLO City News take on all the undesirables who may live among us, nor that Christopher Gardner carry a weapon—as long as he keeps his camera loaded and his vision in focus.

After all, when you start your own newspaper and go after the big picture, it pays to be vigilante.

[August 2006]

Who Is Nelson Waldorf?

Of all the superlative reasons to listen to the Coast Morning Show with Bill Pesso and Amy Jacobs every weekday morning, and they will tell you there are many, few I believe compare with the daily guest appearances of Nelson Waldorf.

Nelson just may be one of the last true rock 'n' rollers, and therefore by default a rebel with a cause. By some incandescent design (probably Amy's but I wouldn't put it past Bill), Nelson has managed to infiltrate KSTT's soft-rock airwaves with the sole purpose of poisoning the minds of its listeners with not only singular recordings of pop/rock music either long since forgotten or never much heard in the first place, but with trivia related to his daily selection earmarked for airplay.

For example, it was just the other day that Nelson played the original version of "California Dreamin,'" which he claims was recorded by ex-folksinger Barry McGuire a few months before the hit by The Mamas and the Papas.

Being somewhat of a Top 40 enthusiast myself, I thought this revelation was, while not profound, certainly intriguing. What other tidbits has Nelson up his sleeve? I am still somewhat afraid to ask, but according to Amy, Nelson is a musicologist with a vinyl collection well into the thousands. "Mostly 45s," I heard Nelson tell Amy, who at first reacted as though Nelson might be some kind of rabid gun nut, until Bill butted in with, "I think Nelson is talking about the little records with the big holes."

If you're a fan as I am of the Coast Morning Show, I'm sure you're aware by now that it's not atypical for Bill to reveal his age as much as Amy does her innocence during any one of their broadcasts. As for Nelson, who has to be as surprised as anyone that he even gets close to a microphone, he's soundly over the hill. But it didn't start out that way.

On the other hand, it probably did.

The way Nelson tells it, he grew up in a home filled with all kinds of popular music. His family favored Broadway show tunes, swing bands, opera, and anything written by Cole Porter or sung by Ray Noble. This musical arena would have to suffice until young Nelson discovered in 1953 among his mother's old and brittle 78s a well-worn campy folk ditty that appealed to his raw and organic nature at the time: "Hallelujah, I'm a Bum."

By the time Elvis came along the following year, Nelson had found his groove, warped as it would become. Much to his mother's chagrin, he started collecting rock 'n' roll and rhythm and blues records. The household hi-fi was soon corrupted, as was the entire household. One rumor has it that when Nelson introduced Little Richard's "Tutti-Frutti" to his mother, she found it necessary to check on the validity of Nelson's birth certificate.

Nelson remained oblivious to all this, of course, unaware that he was kind of like a Cuba sitting off the United States. Despite threats of parental retaliation, Nelson continued to shake, rattle, and roll. There was no known antidote.

For Nelson had discovered, like many other juveniles his age, THE BIG BEAT—that primordial force of the boogie-woogie that absolutely terrified mothers and fathers across the land.

It's no wonder then that Nelson was shipped off to what might as well have been a military school, where proctors quickly confiscated his record player, only to discover the next night that Jerry Lee Lewis was again blaring from Nelson's room. Nelson had gone and bought a record player from a classmate down the hall.

It was not long thereafter that Nelson figured out a way to capitalize on his obsession. He started spinning platters at college fraternity parties and high school hops, which gave him enough spare change to rummage through thrift stores, flea markets and garage sales in search of that rare rock 'n' roll record.

Over the years, as a musician and a disc jockey among other things, Nelson amassed quite an eclectic collection and prided himself on winning rock 'n' roll trivia contests.

He could furnish the answers to questions like "What was Brenda Lee's real name?" or "Name the B-sides to all the Beatles singles" or "Who provided the hand claps in Little Eva's hit song 'The Locomotion'?"

The problem was, as Nelson often learned on street corners waiting to impress passersby, no one really cared. Except his wife, who, thinking of the future, just recently suggested that Nelson stop all his spinning and sell his entire collection.

"Before that happens," says Nelson, "I'm going to transfer all my music to CDs. Now that I've finally found an audience, I plan to Coast for the rest of my life."

[June 2007]

10

Observations

How to recognize you may be coming down with those preverbial holiday blues: You begin to feel ostracized when you realize that your house is the only one on the block that is not decorated with flashing lights and blinking icicles complete with a fully decorated fir tree in the window. So you hang up a wreath on the front door but everyone knows including you that this ain't gonna' cut it.

- Bah Humbug

Nary a Sixpence

I just found out there's at least one other couple that doesn't make a big deal out of Valentine's Day: Michelle and Barack Obama.

They say it's tiresome. That's not the reason in our household.

I made it through another Valentine's Day spending nary a sixpence on the object of my affection, my wife Sara, who not only informed but instructed me some 32 years ago that I need not bother with calling upon Cupid's bow and arrow to ensure our everlasting love for one another, which has always been fine by me.

Not that I was ever off the hook, by any means. During our wedding ceremony on March 17, 1979, immediately after I answered "I do" to the minister's question, "King, do you forever take this woman to be your lawfully wedded wife?" I believe I heard her whisper rather emphatically in my ear something like, "You'd better, buster," which reminded me of the warning shot over the bow courtesy of Buddy Holly, who, when I was an impressionable young lad of 11, once belted out to his lover in song:

> When Cupid shot his dart he shot it at your heart
> so if we ever part then I'll leave you
> you sit and hold me and you tell me boldly
> that someday well, I'll be through
> well, that'll be the day when you say goodbye!

All of which pretty much told me that Sara would prefer receiving my affections every day as opposed to one annual dart every February

14. Or a box of rich chocolates, which would just make her suspicious: "Thank you, sweetness," I can hear her say in her milky way, "But what is it you're really after?" Or an ultra-expensive bunch of long-stemmed red roses: "Don't even think about shelling out 50 dollars for some flowers that will be dead in three days!" Or any kind of racy lingerie, secret or otherwise, which would be totally out of the question and an obvious affront to someone far more like a sophisticated Grace Kelly than, say, a saucy vamp like Theda Bara.

A last-minute stop at the jewelry store would be a desperate attempt at best: "If I want diamonds and pearls, my darling, I'd just as soon wait until our next trip to either Africa or the Far East, and since neither of those is going to happen (along with another trip to Mexico where I might bargain for silver, but since I have gotten sick every time we've been there) I'll settle for something a bit more practical for our 35th wedding anniversary." Which, I better take note, is not all that far away.

As for a simple romantic card, or Valentine, one is always appreciated, but it usually doesn't carry the same impact as a good old-fashioned paycheck.

For those who might think this affair might resemble one without romance, I assure you that it ain't necessarily so. Of course, should the situation ever warrant a spark or two now and then, all you need to do is download a sentimental audio reminder, like the 1962 pop tune out of the Sam Cooke musical catalogue:

> Cupid draw back your bow and let your arrow go
> straight to my lover's heart for me nobody but me
> Cupid please hear my cry and let your arrow fly
> straight to my lover's heart for me.

This being said, I consider myself fortunate that I never have to fear being intimidated by last minute histrionic hucksters who warn of impending doom to the harried man under pressure to deliver. I have also concluded that all those who peddle the necessary holiday wares can't mind too much if I for one opt out.

Last week I read that a fellow who doesn't opt out will spend an average of $111 for a Valentine's Day present this year. My mom would be shocked at the very idea.

"All you need to impress your Valentine is a handmade card," she would often tell me. "A simple query like 'Will you be my Valentine?' written in ink by the hand you don't normally write with so she won't know who it's from, followed by a mysterious 'Guess who?'"

"But Mom, if she doesn't know who it's from, how will she ever know it's from me?"

"Trust me, she'll know."

Years later I'm pretty sure it must have been a note similar to Mom's that I surreptitiously sent to Sara on our very first Valentine's Day. The first thing she said when she received it was, "Boy, King, you sure have lousy handwriting."

Mothers always know, don't they?

As rich as I am for having Sara in my life in the first place, and richer still that I haven't had to buy her something for Valentine's Day every year, I sometimes feel it wise that I remind her of the occasion, just in case she might change her mind sometime in the future.

I'm hoping that the verse from Richard Rogers and Lorenz Hart might do the trick:

> *My Funny Valentine don't change a hair for me*
> *not if you care for me stay, little valentine, stay*
> *each day is Valentine's Day.*

[February 2011]

Monster Mash

Halloween is upon us.

Prepare to be assaulted by all kinds of vampires, werewolves, and other ghost-like creatures that cloves of garlic, religious crosses, and even silver bullets aren't likely to repel. Kids these days, I have found, are impervious not only to all curses but to any remedy that might counteract them, and they will find their way to your door no matter what you do.

Having realized my fate every October 31st, there are a few things I do to get into the spooky spirit of the holiday.

The Pumpkin Patch: Watching youngsters picking out pumpkins bigger than they are is a treat unto itself. Not to be missed is the proverbial scene where a little boy, having bragged to his mates about his strength, picks up a pumpkin just a little too heavy, drops it with a thud to the ground, then looks around to see if anyone saw him do it.

Observant parents, trying to show their kids how to carve a pumpkin, also offer a chuckle considering the offspring usually comes up with a more creative design.

Before leaving the patch, make sure you search for Linus and Lucy. I'm convinced like many others that their patience awaiting the arrival of the Great Pumpkin will be well rewarded.

Costumes: It's a relief to experience that not all costumes that come to your door are those that resemble druids, devils, or diabolical deviants, like a Jason or a Freddy. A little princess is a glorious sight to see, as long as you don't try to guess which princess she claims to be, because if you're wrong, she won't let you forget it. Better to ask, "And what princess might you be?" than declaring, "Oh, you must be Princess Grace," when she's decked out as Princess Diana. The look she gives her mother standing behind might as well express, "Mom, has this guy been left behind or what?"

One other thing about costumes: I don't hand out candy to anyone dressed like a 17-year-old.

Treats: It might be wise to have a vast supply of treats on hand lest you desire to be tricked in one way or another by some mischievous ghoul or goblin. Nothing is worse than the feeling of impending doom should you run low on treats—or worse, run out completely. No kid wants to accept a box of Kraft Macaroni and Cheese in lieu of a Three Musketeers bar.

My advice: Buy too much of what your wife eats.

Song: If you really want to get into the spirit (or spirits) of Halloween, get yourself a copy of "Monster Mash" by Bobby "Boris" Pickett and the Crypt-Kickers, the perennial musical holiday favorite since it topped the charts in October 1962 (a feat, by the way, I find somewhat disquieting, as it was America's number one song right in the midst of the Cuban Missile Crisis).

"Monster Mash," with its infectious beat that resembled the then-current dance craze "The Mashed Potato," and was as novel as "Alley-Oop," became a smash because its singer and author Bobby Picket mimicked Boris Karloff so effectively.

I would bet a bobbed apple that anyone under 50 today has no idea who Boris Karloff is, so it surprises me that it remains a hit. But back in my day we all grew up watching those scary Universal horror films where Bela Lugosi became Dracula, Lon Chaney, Jr. turned into the Wolfman, and Karloff played Frankenstein's monster.

Add these crazy lyrics in the tongue of Boris Karloff to an up-tempo dance number, and how could this not be a Halloween hit? "I was working in the lab late one night when my eyes beheld an eerie sight, for my monster from his slab began to rise, and suddenly to my surprise, he did the Mash, he did the Monster Mash."

Some other verses are just as colorful: "Out from his coffin Drac's voice did ring, seems he was troubled by just one thing, he opened the lid and shook his fist and said, 'Whatever happened to my Transylvania twist?'"

Now there's a Halloween song as well dressed as any Halloween costume, complete with sound effects—a boiling cauldron, a squeaky door, and dragging chains.

Combine it with the resonance of your front doorbell and the giggly chatter of the darling little trolls just outside (all in anticipation of what kind of treats await them) and you'll appreciate another Halloween.

[October 2011]

Fat Chance

As one who has never been all that resolute about resolutions, particularly those that surface every New Year, I see no reason to change my mind this year, even though there are those who no doubt believe my mind is what needs changing the most.

That being said, I will try to keep an open perspective as I peruse the list of things that most people feel they're compelled to accomplish in order to improve their health, their wealth, or their general overall outlook on life. Perhaps there is something here for me, too.

Lose weight. It doesn't surprise me in the least that losing weight is the perennial number one resolution, considering all the feasting we do during the final two months of the year. I for one will admit that all those desserts I rarely eat really did me in this holiday season, to the point where my stomach is now starting to reach my destination before the rest of me. Tell you what: if you think I'm beginning to resemble Warner Brothers' heavy Sydney Greenstreet (*Casablanca, The Maltese Falcon*), I'll think about shedding a few pounds.

Eat right. If I ate right in the first place, losing weight probably wouldn't be an issue at all. But everybody at work knows that's not going to happen, unless I give up my fondness for hot dogs, or macaroni and cheese, or mayo on anything as soon as my radio shift ends at 9 in the morning. All I have to say is thank God there's no In-N-Out Burger in San Luis Obispo. Speaking of beefs, as I'm writing this I can hear my sanctimonious sister (who is the vegetarian queen of the planet) say, "Do you know how much water it takes to produce all the meat from one cow?" Sorry, but I'm just not ready to get sauced on soy. But OK,

I'll try to limit the hot dogs—unfortunate news I'm sure that will not sit well with one of my hungrier co-workers who claims I cook a pretty mean wiener.

Get fit. I do need to get more exercise, so this one resolution I think I can handle: I promised my wife Sara that I'd take our dog Sadie for a daily afternoon stroll that would extend a little further than the mailbox, which is located practically right across the street. I got the feeling recently, however, that more effort might be needed on my part when she handed me a new pair of tennis shoes along with the dictum, "You know it might do you some good to walk around the compound once in a while and see the neighborhood in which we live." Tell you one thing: I'd rather struggle with a few hills than march to the cadence of a thong throng at any fitness center.

Reduce stress. This will be difficult to do unless my mother-in-law misplaces her telephone.

Drink less alcohol. I read way too many stories over the air on KVEC every weekday morning about the perils of drunk driving, so the least I can do is remain the designated driver.

Quit smoking. Mark Twain once said, "Giving up smoking is the easiest thing in the world. I know because I've done it thousands of times." An amusing but not an altogether encouraging remark. But even Mark Twain might be able to quit in this day and age, because soon there will no longer be any place left to smoke and even if you could find one, the habit has become too expensive.

Save money. Impossible. I work in radio.

Get out of debt. See above.

Get more organized. No longer will I use any little yellow stickies.

Find a better job. Right. Try to find ANY job.

Learn something new, like Facebook. Too risky. I have enough addictions already. Or maybe music? Doubtful. I would like to pick up the drums again, except I'm certain my wife would skin me alive if I brought home a pair of bongos. Or a foreign language? Done. I already speak in a language foreign to more than a few.

Take a trip. I'll go as far as Santa Maria to In-N-Out Burger, but I'll be darned if I'm going to get on any airplane, especially with passengers who hide surprises in their underwear.

Volunteer for something. Anything except the U.S. Army.

Be less grumpy. I'm only grumpy when I have to get up at 3:30 every morning. Perhaps getting up at 4 instead might relieve some petulance.

Be more independent. Can't. I'm happily married. (I'd better say this in case my wife reads this, and if she does, it would probably be safer to say "won't" instead of "can't"—otherwise the next 30 years of our union will be miserable, and I can't afford to be any grumpier than I already am.)

Be less skeptical. Who, me? Fat chance.

[January 2010]

Dog Days

I've never seen anything quite like it, and neither have our neighbors.

We have a dog named Sadie who was born to watch the world go by, and that she does, every sunny day, often sitting, but mostly lying down, at the end of our driveway.

From her vantage point, right in front of our garage, she sees all the usual forms of traffic pass by on the busy street in our neighborhood —joggers, walkers, hikers, bikers, horses, and of course all the other neighborhood dogs trotting past with owners in tow.

A couple of things make this picture unusual and amusing: One, Sadie never leaves her post. (Well, that's not entirely true. Whenever she gets too hot, she will pick up and move a few feet and take refuge in the shade.)

And two, she has never been known to bark, howl, or growl. She'll just lie there all day long, lifting her head and cocking her ears when something piques her interest or catches her eye.

And more often than not, it won't be one of the many other colorful canines that are walked by, even those who are feisty, aggressive, or unfamiliar. She pays no mind at all to Big Ben, the bulldog next door, probably because Big Ben looks and behaves more like a bulldozer than a bulldog.

She will give a peculiar glance, however, to the tiny curly-haired white ball of fluff named Smooch that our neighbor Joel walks every day. I think Sadie's idea of a fellow dog is not one you can pick up and hold in your hand.

As curious a hound as Sadie is, and believe me there's a lot to be curious about in our neighborhood, I think she postures herself along the avenue because she mostly desires attention. And she gets more than enough of that.

Motorists in cars will slow, just to see if she's there (they are disappointed if she isn't). Some even stop and get out to pet her, mostly on her tummy because she rolls over as soon as someone approaches.

A few folks have even pulled over and asked me while I'm puttering nearby around the house with my wife Sara, "How in the world did you find such a marvelous animal? Our dog would never stay put. We want a dog like that. Where did you get her?"

As I tell them, we found Sadie at Woods Humane Society eight years ago, when she was about two-and-a-half. We pretty much knew she was the one the moment we spotted her: first, because she was one of the very few dogs in the entire compound who weren't trying to bound out of their pens and barking like the moon was full, and second, because Sadie owned a pair of big brown eyes surrounded by some incredibly beautiful and ornate black and tan markings.

She weighed about 60 pounds and sported a long, pointed tail. We figured her to be some kind of Labrador mix, but if she ever hunted for anything, it was most likely for copious amounts of adoration, which is why Sadie always avoids the back of the house and heads out in front where all the action is, and (upon more occasions than I'd like to admit) food, usually in the form of a biscuit or two, most often provided by our friends Terry and Richard who live right across the street.

Nonetheless I believe it's the sunshine she seeks, to the point of the absurd.

One time I'll never forget, after the sun faded from the driveway, Sadie sneaked to the edge of the still-warm street and rolled on her back, completely still and oblivious, which naturally caught the eye of the next curious motorist who came along.

Thinking Sadie might have been run over, he screeched the brakes, ran to our front door, and panted, "Excuse me, I think your dog may have been hit by a car!"

We all knew she hadn't when her tail started wagging, as it always does when you talk about her, and after thanking the driver, we decided from then on to bring her inside when the sun goes down.

But as sure as the sun rises the next day, after Sara takes her for her morning walk around the neighborhood, Sadie will saunter outside to the front of the house, find the perfect spot for the moment, collapse in sweet surrender, and drift into a world of serenity and comfort known only to her.

That's one trick I'd like to learn.

[July 2008]

Play Ball

Of all the wonderfully curious sounds I love to hear, and there are quite a few—like lifting the lid off a new canister of tennis balls, or opening a bottle of beer (a can isn't bad either but let's face it, suds taste better in glass), or popping a cork off anything—the best is the crack produced by the wood of a bat when it meets a baseball.

Nothing announces the arrival of spring and the promise of summer quite like that particular timbre.

It's also comforting to know that in a restless and troubled world, another season of major league baseball is in full swing, no matter that today I couldn't identify a starting nine—not like I could when I was a kid living in San Francisco after the Giants came to town.

My dad, who was in advertising, helped secure the team's transference from New York by inducing his major client, Folger's Coffee, to sponsor the team on KSFO radio. Consequently, the entire Harris household was constantly tuned to 560 AM, anxiously waiting for announcer Russ Hodges to declare his signature cry—"Bye-bye baby!"—every time a Giant hit a home run.

Going to games was even more of a thrill, of course, despite the cold winds and fog at Candlestick Park. Willie Mays and company were well established by the time the Giants won their first pennant in the fall of 1962, beating the Los Angeles Dodgers in a frenzied playoff to face the New York Yankees in the World Series.

I scrambled to get a ticket for the seventh game of that contest, and was planning to cut high school to go, when I discovered my next door neighbor Ole Olsen, a flyer who lost his leg in the war in the skies over

Germany, had never in his life been to a major league baseball game. So I gave him the pass, and even though the Giants barely lost the game and the series, you couldn't tell it by him upon his return. The experience for Ole was not unlike him having witnessed a game-winning grand slam, a field of dreams come true.

While I personally never had any grand illusions about pursuing baseball as a career, having hometown heroes in my backyard did provide me with a fervent incentive to actively participate in various forms of baseball over the years. Swinging away and mostly striking out on the diamonds I dared during my formative school days, and even those in college (where it seemed that no matter what position I played, the ball would forever fly over my head), later on I got involved in some serious softball with my colleagues at work.

Naturally I preferred slow-pitch to hardball because I always believed that anyone who entered a batter's box facing some out-of-control maniac (who thought he was the next Juan Marichal delivering wildly spinning orbs faster than the speed of jet aircraft) lacked a few brains, and if he didn't, he was about to lose them.

Actually, I couldn't hit all that much in slow-pitch softball, either, but at least I knew what I would encounter the next morning. That is, until the day that Lester joined the team that my Santa Barbara television station KEYT fielded one spring.

Lester was an angry Vietnam vet who played shortstop at the edge of the outfield grass and had the ability to inject his post-war stress into every throw that he made, meaning that if you were on the receiving end of his traumatic tosses, like I was often, playing first base, you'd best pray and light a candle at the Mission should you error in the slightest.

Surviving Lester was one thing, surviving the ire of my wife Sara was another, on that one Saturday I returned home after team practice with an injury to my leg the day before we were to leave for Maui for a long-desired vacation. She was so upset, and rightfully so, that when I told her I had sprained my knee running down a fly ball, she initially suggested in no uncertain terms that I could go to the hospital by myself.

Fortunately, despite my lingering limp, our trip turned out well, but thereafter I wisely decided to hang up my cleats and concentrate instead on viewing the game behind the lens of a camera—until guys like Doug Draper assumed that task.

Doug was one of the best, and perhaps one of the luckiest when it came to shooting high school and college baseball for the sports department. One afternoon he came back with footage that captured a bat-tipped foul ball shattering what we thought was the expensive lens of his KEYT camera, later to learn it was the protective lens cover that got fractured.

Other ABC affiliate news directors having no clue about sports anyway wouldn't know this, of course, so we sent the video ruse to all who, I was told, went apoplectic thinking it was their camera that sustained extensive damage. "You're not playing ball," was their response.

"Never said I could," was my reply.

[April 2010]

What Music They Make

My brother James, that incurable romantic, is up to his old tricks again.

He who once upon a time picked apples in Colorado, drove taxicabs in San Francisco, named his dog Ratso after the Dustin Hoffman character in his favorite movie *Midnight Cowboy*, and christened his future wife Shadow after meeting her in a college tavern while singing "The Shadow of Your Smile," has—not surprisingly—passed on his quixotic characteristics to his children.

Proof of this arrived in the form of a wedding ceremonial request composed by his son Charles and his bride-to-be Horiana Isac, who wanted to get an early word out that family and friends alike were invited to attend their union next August in the homeland of Horiana's Romanian ancestors.

I figured it to be something like this as soon as I spotted the clever subject of their email: "Friends, Romanians, countrymen, lend me your ears."

So I lent them my eyes and read further.

"A message to you all from Charles Harris and Horiana Isac: Servus friends!"

I had to stop reading here to find out what "servus" meant, so I did, and it is Latin for "at your service" or "hello." I continued reading.

"It is happening! I'm not talking about the wedding; I'm talking about the wedding in TRANSYLVANIA!"

Now, that is just about the most romantic spot on the face of the earth.

I've never visited that part of the world, but every time I conjure up images of Transylvania, I don't think of two young lovers getting married. I envision Count Dracula, the king of all vampires, wrapped in a huge black cape, armed with long, dagger-like white teeth dipped in crimson, roaming the countryside in the darkness of night searching for the blood of innocent young virgins or meddling ministers who can't wait to drive a stake through his heart or lure him to sunrise to turn him to dust.

I think of nocturnal bats fluttering through the windows of foreboding, dreary, damp and chilly castles warmed only by candlelight, not far from the local pub where nearby residents soak down the ale while speaking of mysterious lores and legends; unsuspecting travelers who hail the service of a silent coachman who gallops his horse-drawn carriage over pebbled bridges through the darkest of forests; defenseless visitors forced to display wreaths of garlic and the Holy Cross lest they fall victim to the vampire's curse; and the ominous coffin buried in the dank earth of the castle crypt, Dracula's daytime dwelling. And if he's not home, you can expect two small bloody bites on your neck sometime after nightfall.

Perhaps there is more to Transylvania than pictured in all those Hammer horror films I grew up watching. But not much.

"We can visit castles (e.g. chez Dracula), forests, waterfalls, and other medieval cities. In the coming months, you will be formally invited to dance, eat, and otherwise rejoice, but for now we wanted to email you with a date for your planning purposes. Romania may be far from America's friendly shores, the trip long and the adventure taxing on the wallet, but we would love for you to share this moment with us."

Now I'd be the first one to admit that I love to dance, eat, and otherwise rejoice, but I get a little bit anxious about adventures taxing on the wallet, especially when the wallet is mine and it's empty.

And about trips long. Charles and Horiana aren't kidding. "The ultimate destination is Brasov, Romania. There is no airport in Brasov; the closest one is Bucharest—a 2-1/2 hour drive away. Don't worry about getting from Bucharest to Brasov; we will arrange that leg of your journey (a carriage drawn by coal-black horses and driven by a silent coachman will convey you to Brasov). All you have to do is get to Bucharest."

That ought to be easy from San Luis Obispo, if the airline agents even know where Bucharest is. I'll just tell them New York. Horiana can advise me the rest of the way.

"I know of only one direct flight to Bucharest," she relayed. "A direct flight is obviously ideal, but when I go home I typically take a one-stop flight via Frankfurt or Munich. My typical travel time is 7 hours to Germany, a 2-3 hour layover, another 2 hour flight to Romania, and a final 2-1/2 hour drive."

Here I am bothered by the word "final."

It may all be moot. With the way flying is today, if I left San Luis Obispo tomorrow, I'm not sure I'd make it in time for the wedding.

Horiana concludes, "The hard part is getting to Romania; once you are all there, I promise it will be a blast. Imagine watching Charles and me dance our first dance!"

As I listened, I heard as if from down below in the valley the howling of many wolves. The Count's eyes gleamed, and he said: "Listen to them, the children of the night. What music they make!"

[October 2009]

Sympathy from the Devil

What a crazy time we live in.

For example, you lose your job through no fault of your own because of a faltering economy, which is hard enough on your wallet not to mention your psyche, only to get berated for not finding one (when there aren't any) by lawmakers who resist the idea of doling out unemployment insurance during the worst recession since the Great Depression.

And God forbid you protest your plight, because if you do, you'll be criticized by pathetic television pundits who label you as too lazy, too particular, and even un-American.

One of these blowhards the other day went so far (as he constantly does) to suggest "Don't spend your remaining money on travel to get to a protest. Go out and get a job. You may not want the job. Work at McDonald's. Work two jobs. There has been plenty of times in my life I've done jobs I hated, but I had no choice. Two years is plenty of time to have lived off your neighbor's wallet."

Referring to people who have exhausted the unprecedented 99 weeks of unemployment benefits, he asked, "Have you heard of the 99ers? Some of these people, I bet you'd be ashamed to call them Americans."

How appropriate. Sympathy from the devil.

I can tell you first-hand that being without work, known as "on the beach" in my business, is no barrel of laughs, no matter what the economic conditions. And not only do the folks down at the unemployment office keep tabs on your search efforts but they hold mandatory seminars to guide you through the process. Failure to undertake either one often results in your benefits being severed.

One of the things I learned over the years is that if you create movement for yourself, like volunteering for a nonprofit organization like United Way, you will meet a lot of people who either have or know about job opportunities you might be interested in and even if you're not, at least you are aware of them and it gives you more choices.

If you are persistent, most likely you will eventually land something, which I did in 2008 when I convinced KVEC news director Ben Greenaway that I could forgive the owner of the station (Clear Channel) for demoting me several years earlier for sounding "too folksy" over the air.

As for employment for the sake of a paycheck, I think just about everybody has worked at a job or two they didn't like. There are several in my past.

One was in construction where I learned how to dig a pretty mean ditch with blisters to prove it, but I did help build the Coffee Contada restaurant on Union Street in San Francisco that was used in the Steve McQueen movie *Bullit*.

Another was at a lithography plant where I was stationed at the end of a relentless assembly belt packaging endless labels for canned goods.

Then there was the proverbial gas station, where if I wasn't trying to put brakes on some guy's car, I was forever pumping petrol while scraping bugs off some trucker's windshield.

My favorite job I liked the least was working at Woolworth's, where I managed the record department, which was OK since I'm into music and all, but having to sell goodies at the candy counter at noon and filling up helium balloons for the kids non-stop was not my idea of a promising career.

How I got into television news is another story entirely, but I will tell you I was surprised when KEYT in Santa Barbara decided not to renew my contract in 1997 after a successful run as news director and anchor for almost 20 years. That led to my first experience with the unemployment office, and to an adventure I'll never forget.

While wondering what to do or where to go next, I was approached by my friend Walter Capps, who had just won a seat in the House of Representatives. He asked me if I'd like to be his assistant in Washington, D.C. I answered with an enthusiastic yes, and told him I'd find a way to pay for the trip myself.

So in the winter of 1997, I traveled to the Beltway, arriving at the train station where I changed into a suit in the men's room, a frightening procedure I don't recommend to anyone since the stalls are filled with pill-pushers, drug addicts, and people with no birth records.

After trudging through a cold rain to the halls of Congress, I met with Walter's staff who concluded that I was overqualified for the position after wincing at my conviction that I was going to change the way things were done in the nation's capitol.

Determined nonetheless, I proceeded to look for places to live, and called my wife Sara, advising her that we were going to move.

Ultimately, after writing Walter's first words to Congress, I realized (as did Sara) that getting involved in the unalterable political scene was a tenuous move at best, so I respectfully declined the offer.

What did I learn? Job searching can be one hell of a trip.

[August 2010]

Bah Humbug

How to recognize you may be coming down with those preverbial holiday blues:

You start feeling guilty when people that you haven't heard from in years keep sending you Christmas cards that you know you're never going to answer (not even to ask the ages of their children who have grown so remarkably) yet they never take you off their list.

You get cranky when the only songs they play on nearly every radio station in town are nothing but Christmas carols.

You get irritated when the neighbor across the street who never had an unhappy or unpleasant Christmas moment in his whole life hangs up flashing lights and blinking icicles complete with a fully decorated fir tree in the window—two weeks before Thanksgiving.

You begin to feel ostracized when you realize that your house is the only one on the block that is not decorated with flashing lights and blinking icicles complete with a fully decorated fir tree in the window. So you hang up a wreath on the front door but everyone knows including you that this ain't gonna' cut it.

You feel obligated into going to the office Christmas party because if you don't you may not be working come January first. This brings on other concerns, provided you do attend. Like you may have too much to drink and say something to somebody (such as your boss) that you know you're going to regret, like, "Why does our party have to be on a Sunday night?" thereby putting yourself in the position of being out of work long before January first.

You haven't done a lick of Christmas shopping nor do you have any desire to, but you do begin to feel empathy toward the woman who pepper-sprayed her competing shoppers at a big box store.

You wince at even the remotest thought of going to any family gatherings because the dysfunction that exists every other day of the year is only going to be worse when everybody's forced upon one another as they always are in the guise of being cheerful and supportive.

You cringe every time you pass by a Salvation Army bell ringer, especially the one who is new to the job and wants to prove she was worth the hire by ringing four bells (not one) in two fists with so much zeal that you can't believe her arms haven't yet separated from her shoulders.

You tire easily of trying to figure out what Yuletide greeting to offer, be it "Merry Christmas" or "Happy Holidays" or "Season's Greetings," because if it's the wrong one (according to those with politically correct sensitivities), you will have insulted someone who probably does not nor never has cared a second thought about it.

Of course, if you do offend someone offering good tidings and good will, you risk being slighted should you exclaim, "Peace be with you, brother," which can get a response like, "I'm not your brother and what are you anyway, a Communist?"

[December 2011]

Recovery

Where the heck have I been these past few months?

I'd like to tell you I've been trotting around the globe visiting some paradisiacal distant lands like Machu Picchu, Bora Bora, Majorca, Maui, or Puerto Vallarta perhaps.

But no, in the dream I had to have been in, I selected Lompoc, a flat and windy Central Coast town which is hard to find and even harder to get out of. Friendly residents there will tell you there's nothing much to do in Lompoc, and they'd be right.

Still, there are some varied sights to see. For those of you interested in the saga of California Missions, might I suggest the beautifully restored La Purisima which sits under sunny skies in nearby open fields.

If you enjoy exploring the criminal mind, you could stop by the imposing Federal Correction facility down the road.

If you are a fan of Hollywood and cinema, the Lompoc Theater Project is underway.

For all other addictions, head on over to "C" Street where you will find a rather new health facility called the Champion Center, which prides itself in its successful treatment for those whose lives have become overstressed and unmanageable.

After having been in the crazy and zany world of the news business for nearly four decades, and after having spent a year in Vietnam in the late sixties, it's not too difficult to figure out where I spent most of my time in Lompoc. Realizing that trauma and alcohol were now my foes, it was the Veterans Administration that sent me to the Champion Center for 60 days, starting at the end of February.

First stop, top floor, the medical unit, which is staffed by a bevy of eager nurses who watch you like a hawk (not ever letting you out of their sight), and a cadre of serious doctors who examine you every morning.

Don't plan on getting any kind of consistent sleep in this unit while you endlessly wait for your head to clear; the nurses make sure they take your blood pressure what seems like every 15 minutes.

If there's a class to take or food to eat from the cafeteria, both offered downstairs, a nurse with what may be a leash will accompany you every step of the way.

Trust me. There is no way to escape the nurses.

Unless of course, you are fortunate enough to have graduated (getting a clean bill of health) to more private living quarters on the first floor, which also houses classrooms, counselors, and administration.

As for the curriculum, Champion primarily focuses on a 12-step program for those patients who need treatment for addictions such as drug dependency or alcohol abuse.

For such situations, tools for addictive behavior are provided as are any signs of triggers that may steer an individual off course. Students also learn about the value of diet and nutrition, which must be an important part of recovery, judging by the nature and amount of the food served up by the cafeteria, where three meals a day of mystery dishes are mandatory.

And by the way, if you find yourself in need of a jolt in the morning, or anytime for that matter, you won't get it on the premises from coffee or any other caffeinated beverage.

Exercise is also heavily encouraged to get the body back in shape. Walking or hiking is popular, and Champion has access to a nearby gym and swimming pool which are taken advantage of several times a week.

Even yoga and meditation, both excellently orchestrated by a resilient and spiritual woman named Bob (yes, Bob), play a strong part in getting back to a healthy mind, body, and soul.

When you aren't in the classroom, that usually indicates a trip to a local A.A. or N.A. meeting is in store.

Champion doesn't fool around. The days are long and crowded, from 7 in the morning until sometimes 9 at night. And there are enough rules to obey that sometimes you might mistake the experience for either some kind of boot camp or honor farm.

But if you're in need of direction towards the straight and narrow, the Champion Center is more than a beneficial way to spend your time.

It may even save your life.

[March 2017]

11

Edgar and Willoughby

Edgar and Willoughby, the two giant, burly Alaskan bull moose who once upon a time (in the not too distant past) were forced to meet secretly in clandestine locations for fear of being hunted from the air by their former gun-toting' governor (whose fervent desire for moose stew constantly had them on the run), could now gather casually around their favorite watering hole out in the open without worry.

- Moose Jaw Popcorn

With Huntley

Moose Jaw

It's not easy being a moose in Alaska.

No one knows that better than Edgar and Willoughby, two weathered and surly old bulls who have survived everything from earthquakes, avalanches, and global warming, to Kodiak attacks, wolf packs, picture-hungry tourists, helicopter hunters, and the current governor, lovingly referred to by the moose in the region as Annie-O (short for Annie Oakley), whose fondness for a warm, hearty plate of moose stew after a strenuous day of snow machining has now become well-known far beyond state boundaries—ever since she set her sights on the second highest office in the land with nary a blink.

"I tell you, Willoughby, it's cause for celebration," Edgar told his longtime friend, as the pair peacefully grazed in an open meadow, surrounded by tall trees in a remote spot in the vast hinterlands of the midnight sun. "We're free at last."

"Not so fast, Edgar. We're not out of the woods yet," replied Willoughby. "They don't serve up much moose on the campaign trail, and you know how ravenous she gets. I'm sure she's got her Huey on standby for another sortie."

Edgar and Willoughby hadn't spoken to each other all that much recently, because ever since Annie-O was elected governor two years ago, it hadn't been safe for one big bull moose to be out in the open, much less two. But the wise and wily Edgar believed they could dare to be a bit bolder these days, certain that her hunger to serve the nation would replace the one she had for moose burgers.

Willoughby, on the other hand, was much more cautious, and

perhaps had reason to be. Over the past several years he had developed a sore knot in his neck from constantly looking upward into the skies overhead, searching for any sight or sound of the strange looking whirlybirds loaded with trigger-happy trophy hunters, including Annie-O, scouring the barren landscape for his hide or his head. Every time Willoughby stretched overhead to munch a leaf or two from a birch tree, an excruciating pain reminded him of his lingering paranoia.

"I still believe you're much too brazen these days, Edgar, walking around in the open like this, making yourself a nice fat target. For all you know, she could fly overhead any minute now with that Austrian rifle of hers and pop you right between your antlers."

Edgar, ever taking things in stride, tried to reassure his sometimes-petrified pal. "I really don't think we have all that much to worry about, Willoughby. For one thing, she'll find it difficult to sneak up on us anymore. She can't go anywhere in those crazy heels of hers without reporters doggin' her every step. And my guess is that if she does get time to come back home, she'll skate a few rinks with her family, and then head westward to Nome to wave at the Russians across the straights."

"She still doing that?"

"More than ever, my dear Willoughby, now that she has to brush up on foreign affairs. She's more under the gun than we are."

"I'm still apprehensive, Edgar. What if Annie-O gets her gun and wants to engage in an aerial moose patrol for the whole world to see?"

"I still think we're safe, Willoughby. Perhaps more secure than before. It wouldn't look good, her taking pot shots at the official state animal. Besides, she's ordered everyone to shoot at all the wolves that attack us moose."

"But wolves don't make a good stew after a strenuous day of snow machining. Can't you see what she's doing, Edgar? Less wolves equals more moose equals more moose meat. And the more I think about it, the more my neck hurts."

"Settle down, my dear Willoughby, there's no reason to panic. Annie-O is off and running for prime time. She's no longer walking that road to nowhere. She's aiming for bigger game, and she's got all those braying beltway donkeys in her crosshairs."

"But all the publicity she's been getting is so unsettling, Edgar. Not in my wildest dreams did I believe she'd become such a hit, and overnight, at that. She's making us moose as famous and fashionable as the shoes, the glasses, and the do. We're in vogue. Why just yesterday I opened up the newspaper, and there she was in one of those cartoons, showing her straddling a snorting, rip-roaring moose, with one hand waving a shotgun and another holding a sign that says, 'The buck could stop here.' That's rather presumptuous, don't you think?"

"For once you're right on target, Willoughby. But I gotta take my horns off to her. She's got plenty of guts."

"Yeah, as long as she's not after mine."

[October 2008]

Moose Jaw Revisited

Edgar and Willoughby, the two burly Alaskan moose who were once a favorite target of the state's governor before she set her sights on bigger game last year, were lumbering down a winding mountain trail on their way to their favorite watering hole.

Both the old bulls had felt it a much safer climate in recent months to travel out in the open as a pair because Annie-O (short for Annie Oakley) had been much too distracted and preoccupied to go moose hunting. As a matter of fact, Edgar and Willoughby weren't sure that Annie-O could even find her moose-hunting gear anymore; they figured by now it was most likely buried under countless stylish sets of formal dresswear bestowed upon her by a party more loyal to an elephant.

"What a relief that is," sighed Willoughby. "I can't very well see her trying to chase us down wearing bright red open-toed pumps."

"Let's never underestimate the old girl, my dear Willoughby," Edgar responded cautiously. "You just never know what she's going to do next."

"Like suddenly resigning in the middle of her first term?" queried Willoughby.

"Exactly that, my good friend," replied Edgar. "She's always locked and loaded, ready to fire. The next time Annie-O gets her gun, I hope she's aiming for targets other than us moose."

"There's obviously no shortage in that department, Edgar," Willoughby agreed, hoping to console his old-time friend. "She might even run out of ammo. David Letterman alone might be worth more than a full clip."

Nonetheless, in between sips of lake water, Edgar still expressed his concern. Because of Annie-O's perpetual thirst for surprise, her raven-ous and well-known hunger for a hearty bowl of Alaskan moose stew might actually increase. Willoughby suggested that what she had on her plate right now might be too full for that.

"For one thing, Edgar, she has a growing family to take care of. For another, she's got a mountain of legal expenses to pay, and she's under the gun herself to write a book to help eliminate those. She's going to be too busy to chase after us."

"We mustn't get complacent, Willoughby. With all the money she's going to make writing that book, she can pay off the lawyers, and have more than enough left over to buy her very own moose-hunting whirly-bird. I tell you, Willoughby, the woman is a barracuda. She even said so herself."

Edgar prided himself on his ability for recall, but in this case he didn't have to strain. A few days after Annie-O first dropped her breathless bombshell on the eve of Independence Day, she met with a puzzled press in a second news conference trying to explain what she meant by the first.

She had initially described her leaving Alaska by using a basketball analogy: "The great State of Alaska and her great people know what I was talking about last Friday. But let me explain again to those who are eager to attack me. When I was a point guard at Wasilla High School, my nickname was The Barracuda. Barracudas hunt in packs and they put on a full-court press on their prey, just like people have been doing to me. And driving to the hoop, this barracuda didn't want to succumb because if I let them beat me, I'd be like a dead fish floating in the cur-rent. But that's not how this barracuda is wired. No siree. Barracudas know when to pass the ball—for victory. Or at least they would if they had hands underwater there, instead of fins and whatnot."

Willoughby almost choked drinking all this in, other than the lake he was lapping. "I'll never understand that woman," he sputtered.

"What's the matter, Willoughby? You look like you just saw a barra-cuda in the water you're sipping," Edgar mused.

Willoughby adroitly stepped away from the pond. "Edgar, you're frightening me. You think Annie-O is stepping down to step up. You think she's off to the Beltway, don't you?"

"It's the perfect place for a predator, Willoughby. She'll be right at home, swimming amongst a battery of barracudas. And if she stays out of foul trouble, she might even make it to the top."

"You mean to tell me, Edgar, that despite her lack of office, with all her political conflicts, and all her legal problems, and all her family trials, and her waning popularity, Annie-O is going to run for President?"

"One can only hope, my dear Willoughby. I for one would just rather see her hunting big game in Washington. Wouldn't you?"

[July 2009]

Moose Jaw Popcorn

Edgar and Willoughby, the two giant, burly Alaskan bull moose who once upon a time (in the not too distant past) were forced to meet secretly in clandestine locations for fear of being hunted from the air by their former gun-totin' governor (whose fervent desire for moose stew constantly had them on the run), could now gather casually around their favorite watering hole out in the open without worry.

Ever since her nomination for Vice President, the ex-mayor of Wasilla, whom Edgar and Willoughby always referred to as Annie-O (short for Annie Oakley), now hungered for political power as opposed to moose meat.

"I do believe, my good friend Willoughby, that for at least the next couple of years anyway, we're pretty much in the clear," noted Edgar, an observation that relieved his old-time companion.

"Do you think, Edgar, she actually is going to make a run for President?" wondered Willoughby.

"Well, Willoughby, all the signs are there. She's on a nationwide bus tour, she's written a couple of books, she just made a movie due out soon, and she's bought a house in Arizona."

"But is she capable?" asked Willoughby. "I find her version of American history rather skewed, don't you?"

"I assume you refer to her recent account of Paul Revere's ride, where she claimed 'Paul Revere warned the British that they weren't going to be taking away our arms, by ringing those bells and making sure as he was riding his horse through town to send those warning shots and bells that we were going to be secure and we were going to be free.'"

"That's the one," said Willoughby. "I always thought Revere warned the colonials, not the English."

"According to factual legend, Willoughby, Revere (who by the way did not ring any of those bells or fire any warning shots) was riding to warn rebels Samuel Adams and John Hancock that they were about to be arrested."

"Edgar, how could she assert otherwise when she claimed 'You know what? I didn't mess up about Paul Revere. Here is what Paul Revere did. He warned the Americans that the British were coming, and they were going to try to take our arms. And part of Paul Revere's ride—and it wasn't just one ride—he was a courier, he was a messenger. Part of his ride was to warn the British that we're already there. That, hey, you're not going to succeed. You're not going to take American arms. You are not going to beat our own well-armed persons, individual, private militia that we have. He did warn the British. And in a shout-out, gotcha type of question that was asked of me, I answered candidly. And I know my American history.'"

"Well, Willoughby, that's a good shout-out, gotcha type question. Kind of like the one where Annie-O, when asked who her favorite fore-father was, responded with, 'All of them.'"

"I guess we can expect to learn a lot more about our heritage while she's on that infamous Rolling Thunder bus tour of hers."

"Consider it similar to the ride of Paul Revere, Willoughby. A warning."

"Should we be concerned that her tour might include Alaska?"

"I don't think so, Willoughby. Folks hereabouts aren't too happy with her, jumping ship and all. My guess is that she'll eventually motor on into Scottsdale and park it inside her 8,000-square foot stucco-style 4.4-acre walled and gated compound she just bought for one-million-seven, which includes grand entry ceilings complete with gourmet kitchen, private home theater, billiard game room, walk-in wine closet, expansive living room, and resort-style backyard with a large gazebo, and pool, of course."

"How about that," cried Willoughby. "She and John McCain are practically neighbors. Do you suppose they will visit each other, Edgar?"

"By the time they do, Willoughby, Annie-O will have become a Hollywood legend. The new documentary film in which she stars, *The Undefeated*, will most likely have hit theater screens nationwide.

"From what I've heard, it follows Annie-O's time as governor, her run for vice-president, and her current political life. The reviews so far are enough to make me want to see it.

"Let me read to you from the New York Post: 'Its tone is an excruciating combination of bombast and whining, it's so outlandishly partisan that it makes Richard Nixon look like Abraham Lincoln, and its febrile rush of images, not excluding earthquakes, car wrecks, volcanic eruption and attacking Rottweilers, reminded me of the brainwash movie Alex is forced to sit through in *A Clockwork Orange*. Except no one came along to refresh my pupils with eyedrops.'

"Now let me read to you from CBS news: 'If you like Alaska's former governor, the movie will make you like her even more. Using never-before seen video, it shows her taking on the machine and winning, while racking up whopping 80 percent approval ratings in the state. And you will feel fresh outrage about how savagely she has been treated and mocked by Hollywood and the liberal elite.'"

"I don't know, Edgar. It sounds more like a Roger Corman b-picture."

[June 2011]

Acknowledgements

Cover by Erin Ambrose.
Cover photograph by Chris Gardner.
All other photographs courtesy of the author.
Printed by SLOCO Data & Printing, Grover Beach, California.
Edited by Charlotte Alexander.

Thanks to all the fine people who have worked and who continue to toil in local media everywhere, covering community news and events, including SLO City News, Tolosa Press, New Times, KMST, KEYT, KCOY, KSBY, KVEC, and SLO Review.

About the Author

King Harris was a native Californian, raised in the country town of Woodside and the city of San Francisco. During his youth, King much preferred rock 'n' roll music to anything that local grade and high schools had to offer, yet he somehow graduated to college where he was disappointed to learn that being a Top 40 disc jockey or a drummer in a rock band weren't part of the school curriculum. King's subsequent choice to major in English caught the attention of Uncle Sam, who in 1969 sent him to Vietnam as a Defense Language Instructor. Not long after his release, he discovered the world of journalism in Steinbeck Country, a craft and occupation he vigorously explored for more than four decades all along the Central Coast of California, sharing his adventures and accolades with his beloved wife Sara. King died in 2022.

ItsGoodToBeKingHarris.com